Kick Her Ag ish

Kick Her Again; She's Irish

Mary and Colin O'Reiley

Kick Her Again; She's Irish
Fourth Edition 2013

ISBN-13: 978-1475126594

ISBN-10: 147512659X

Distributors and retailers can purchase this book directly from the publisher at:
www.createspace.com/info/createspacedirect

In Loving Memory of Marie

PROLOGUE
Mary O'Reiley

Almost twenty years ago, I sat down with a tape recorder and the youngest members of my husband's family and asked them to tell me the story of their childhood. And thus began one of the most fascinating evenings of my life. I could have listened to them all night. But what strikes me the most now, as I look back on that evening so many years ago, was the wonderful sense of joy and good humor emanating from all of them. The O'Reiley family laughs a lot. And it's not a laughter that makes fun of others, but a laughter that shows us the absurdities of life. It's a laughter that wants to gather everyone around to share in it.

But the laughter also puzzled me. How could they laugh about such a traumatic childhood? Then I realized that people who grow up in these types of stressful environments have a choice when they finally claw their way out of them. They can hold on to their grievances and let their childhood ruin their adult lives or they can let them go and laugh about it. The O'Reileys have chosen laughter. After growing up as they did, they know they can survive anything.

This book is the result of that night so long ago. While the names and places in the stories have been changed to protect the identities and privacy of the people involved, these are the stories I heard that night.

Also, I would like to mention that I, and the other members of my family, do not agree with some of the sentiments and the hatred expressed in the chapters on racial tension, including the remarks made by the teacher called Mrs. Johnson. I am just telling the stories as they actually happened. This is, after all, a true story.

THE O'REILEY FAMILY

Mother:	Marie
Father:	Henry
Stepfather:	Joe
Grandmother:	Nana
Children oldest to youngest:	Daniel
	John
	Amy
	Eric
	Sean
	Katie
	Colin
Amy's husband:	Stuart
Amy's son:	Evan
John's wife:	Sheri
Colin's wife:	Mary
Marie's sister-in-law:	Aunt Helen
Marie's brother:	Uncle Milton

The story begins in an impoverished section of Miami, Florida, in the 1960s........

COLIN

Mom was screaming at the world again. She was in the yard in her blue-flowered dress, no shoes. Fists raised to a deaf and indifferent summer sky. A flood of profanity powered by her lungs filled the night. Our neighbor, Mr. Green, had heard it all before.

"Shut up Mrs. O'Reiley!"

Mom directed her barrage in his direction and the war of words was on again. Across the street, lights in the projects flicked on randomly. Faces filled the windows. The curious and nosy were up to watch the show.

I knelt at the window, rubbing sleep from my eyes. Next to me were two of my six brothers and sisters, Sean and Katie. Silently, with lights flashing, the police arrived–three cars and a paddy wagon. Mr. Green must have called them. Mom now had a new target for her verbal assault. Three cops approached her. They jingled and clanged into the yard, feeling for their batons and checking their holsters. Streetlight reflected off their handcuffs.

Mom sat down and continued to curse as if anticipating a confrontation.

"Get up Mrs. O'Reiley and walk to the wagon."

"No you needle dick the bug fucker!" My Mom could swear like no one I've ever met.

They grabbed her arms and dragged her toward the street.

"I'll get up!" she shouted and started to rise.

They knocked her down and dragged her some more.

"Get up Mrs. O'Reiley."

"No! You'll knock me down again! You son of a bitch!"

"Get up!"

My mother tried to stand up, but a cop hit her on the shoulders with a baton. Down she went.

"Get up!"

Mom let loose with a combination of swear words never heard before or since in one sentence.

"You God-damn, mother-fucking, baby-raping, son-of-a-bitch, blue-balled bastards!"

They hit her again.

My fourteen-year-old brother, Eric, who had been hiding across the street, couldn't hold back any longer. He ran from the shadows and jumped on the back of the nearest cop as he screamed, "Leave my mother alone!"

Eric tried to gouge the cop's eyes out. Another cop grabbed him and threw him into the paddy wagon.

My mother kept up her defiance. The cops continued to beat her until they forced her into the paddy wagon.

They drove away. The night was quiet again except for the sobs that came from my throat. Silent tears dripped down Katie's eyes and Sean's lips quivered as he clenched his fists.

We looked at each other, not knowing what to do. They'd never taken her away before. Usually they'd just given her a warning and left. We were all alone.

Luckily for us, we had kind neighbors. A family from down the street took us to their house, and we spent the rest of the night sleeping on their floor. They gave us breakfast at Royal Castle. I loved those little burgers.

Two days later Mom returned home, all battered black and blue.

AMY

I was not living at home when my Mom was beaten by the police, so I'm not exactly sure why she was outside screaming at the world. I don't think it was any one incident that triggered it, but it may have been her whole life leading up to that moment. She had a lot to scream about.

It all started one perfect summer day when Mom and some of her girlfriends decided to swim across a lake near where they grew up in Massachusetts. . . .

"Hey, Marie, I bet you can't swim across the lake!"

"I can too! It's only about a mile. That's not so far!"

"Let's all go! It'll be fun!"

And so the swim that would change the course of my Mom's life began, or at least that's how I imagine it began. About halfway across the lake Mom started getting tired, dangerously tired. She and her friends started to panic.

"Help! Help! Someone help us!" They frantically looked around the lake for assistance.

And there he was, their knight in shining armor, in the form of a very handsome dark-haired, green-eyed young man paddling a canoe toward them. He and Marie took one look at each other and it was love at first sight.

At least, that's how I imagine it happened. Of course, they are *my parents, so I can imagine the story however I want to. . . .*

Marie and Henry started dating. It was all so care free; those were innocent times back then. They went to dances and parties, double dating with Marie's brother, Milton, and Henry's sister, Helen. And on one romantic, moonlit night Henry proposed to Marie in the canoe that had brought them together.

Henry bought a house six months before the wedding, and his future father-in-law helped him get it ready for the newlyweds. Everything was perfect. Love abounded, and the fairy-tale story had its happy ending. Oh, and by the way, Milton and Helen got married also!

DANIEL

"Hey, Marie! Help the kids get packed! We're moving to Florida!" Dad yelled as he burst through the door. He'd stopped for a quick drink after work and was weaving slightly. Lately it seemed as if Mom and Dad were drinking more and more.

"What do you mean, moving to Florida?" Mom looked at him in astonishment.

"I'm sick of working in this cold weather. It's time we moved to a place where I can work year round."

Dad was a carpenter and had spent the winter before doing construction in Florida, so he knew there was work to be had there. Within three days, he and Mom packed their belongings in a trailer, said goodbye to their relatives, shoved us four kids into the old Buick, and headed south.

We were driving through the Smoky Mountains. There was no one else around for fifty miles. Mom, Amy, Eric, and I were singing "On Top Of Old Smoky," and John was off in his own world playing with his model airplanes. All of a sudden, the car sputtered to a stop. We quit singing and looked at each other. Dad got out of the car and opened the hood.

Mom said brightly, "Don't worry kids, your Dad can fix anything that moves!"

I decided to get out to see what was happening. I went over to where Dad was peering at the engine.

"What's going on?" I asked.

"There's something wrong with the points." Dad replied. He stared off into space for a moment and then poked his head through the car window

"John, let me borrow your airplane for a minute." He examined the plane and then turned to Mom. "Marie, can you get me some thread from your sewing kit?"

Mom rummaged around in the trunk and found him some thread. I watched as Dad broke off a small metal piece from the airplane and secured it with thread to the distributor.

"Marie, try to start the engine."

Mom turned the key, and the engine roared. We kids let out a cheer. Our Dad could fix anything!

COLIN

The house that my family moved into in Florida was in northwest Miami. Across the street were the Projects: row after row and block after block of red roofs and dirty white walls. My Aunt Helen, Uncle Milton, and their thirteen children lived in the projects. I think my parents bought our house there so we could be near them. In the fifties the Projects were filled with poor white trash. I think we were white trash too, but we had a house, actually a duplex, and a huge yard on a corner lot. We would rent out one side to help pay the bills while we lived in the other half. Fifteen coconut trees ran along the border of our yard and the streets. One could see the stumps where there used to be more, but every time there was a hurricane, we would lose one or two. A big Banyan tree filled a large part of the front yard with huge branches and side roots that stretched to the ground. We even had a lawn that took Sean most of a day to mow.

Next door was the Salvation Army church and a house where the preacher, Mr. McCarvey, lived. He worked out with weights. Strength for Jesus. He would let all the kids in the neighborhood hang around and work out if they came to church on Sundays. The bribe worked, and for a while we went to his church instead of our own Catholic church. Mr. McCarvey was also a wannabe actor, so he would act out all the parts of his sermons. It was very funny stuff and sometimes very scary–especially when he played the part of the devil. Hellfire and Brimstone all over the pulpit! The pews of his church were always full–standing room only. I even convinced Mom to go. She loved it. Katie and I got so involved that we would go with the Salvation Army Band on Wednesday nights and march through the Projects singing "Bringing in the Sheep" at the top of our lungs. Singing for Jesus. That summer we went to a Salvation Army camp, and I was saved, at least until fall.

AMY

Once we moved to Florida, it seemed as if Mom and Dad were drinking *all* of the time. I wanted them to stop drinking. It made them fight too much. Mom was always calling Dad names and screaming at him.

I could hear them at night, Mom saying "Nah, Nah, Nah, Nah, Nah," and Dad probably saying all of the wrong things, "Marie, Marie, calm down."

I covered my head so I wouldn't hear it, but it never seemed to work. I wished we had stayed in Massachusetts

AMY

The night Mom went to the hospital I cried all night. I will never forget what happened that day. I was sitting at the sewing machine in the kitchen, making an apron for Mom, when she burst through the back door crying and moaning.

"NOOOOOOO, NOOOOOO. How could he do this to me?"

I'd never seen her look so sad. Her face was puffed up and red, tears were running down her cheeks, and she sobbed, crying over and over, "Why, why, why? How could he do this, and with that *bitch*, why?"

"Mom, what's wrong, what happened?" I shook her shoulder.

She sobbed. "Your father, he slept with Flo next door."

"Daddy. . .Daddy slept with Flo?"

Mom just nodded her head and kept crying.

Seeing my Mom cry made me so sad that I put my head down and started crying too.

When I looked up, Mom had left the room. I could hear her sobbing and rummaging around in the bathroom.

"That tart, that bitch, I'll show her. I thought she was my friend!"

I heard drawers opening and closing, and then utter silence.

"Mom? Mom, what are you doing?"

"I'll show her, that bitch."

Mom rushed out of the bathroom. I saw a flash of red coming from her wrists as she raced by me out the door. I ran after her.

The memory of what happened next will always be with me. Mom, her slashed wrists bleeding, was waving them back and forth, smearing blood across the windows of the house next door where Flo lived. "You bitch, you're taking my husband, you've ruined my life, come out here and wash my blood!" She was going back and forth waving her wrists against the windows. "Come out and wash my blood, wash my blood. . . ."

It was the most horrible thing I've ever seen. I didn't know what to do. I ran across the street to the projects to find my aunt Helen. Luckily, she was home and came rushing back to the house with me. She took Mom in her arms and comforted her, leading her into the kitchen. Mom had to go to the hospital to have her arms stitched up, and they've kept her for observation for a few days.

Dad came home looking sheepish and embarrassed to find Mom gone.

JOHN

There was a huge party at Flo's house one afternoon, complete with music, booze, and dancing. We could hear it throughout the neighborhood. Flo invited Dad to the party. Mom was still in the hospital from slashing her wrists. Maybe if she'd been home, Dad wouldn't have taken Flo up on her invitation. I'm not sure why Dad even went, the whole neighborhood knew by then that Flo and Dad were sleeping together, including Flo's husband Hank.

I was in the house watching TV when my little brother Sean came running in.

"John! John! There's a fight at Flo's, and they're beating up Dad! Hurry! They're hurting him, hurry!" Sean grabbed my arm and started pulling me toward the door.

I followed him into the back yard and saw that two young Marines, relatives of Hank's, had pinned Dad against the white picket fence separating our yard from Flo's. One guy was holding him while the other punched him again and again, saying, "That's what you get. . .(punch). . .for sleeping with another. . .(punch). . .man's wife. . .(punch)."

I didn't even stop to think. I rushed over, grabbed the arm of the Marine holding Dad, and pulled it through to our side of the fence. Once I had the arm through the fence, I twisted it backwards as hard as I could until I heard the bone give a sharp "Crack." The guy let out a high-pitched scream of agony. No one seemed to hear it over the loud party music coming from the house.

Now that there was only one Marine to contend with, Dad was able to get up and continue the fight. He punched the remaining Marine in the face and managed to vault over the fence and get away. I picked up Sean and ran back into the house. The last thing I saw was the white face of the Marine staring after me, holding his broken arm.

COLIN

My earliest memories of growing up within a "normal" two-parent family don't include my father's image, just the echo of footprints he left behind. Although I was only two years old when he left, I can still hear the end of normal. I would hide with Sean and Katie under the blanket that covered the TV–our only safe haven from the storm that raged in the rest of the house. I don't recall the words, just the flavor lingers. The blanket wasn't thick enough or the TV loud enough to cocoon us from the end.

AMY

Dad moved to the Virgin Islands and left us behind in Florida. He already had a job down there, and I guess since he and Mom hadn't been getting along, he decided to leave us for good. No one wanted him to go, not even Mom. She did everything she could think of to try to get him to stay. She even told Eric that Dad didn't love him anymore. I guess she thought if Dad saw us kids upset, maybe he wouldn't leave.

I listened to Dad and Eric talking about it in the backyard. Eric was crying his eyes out, and Dad was saying, "Of course I still love you! I don't know why your mother said that! You can come to visit me in the islands once I get settled. I'll always love you." Eric kept crying and crying and crying. . . .

Little Colin was only two years old and didn't know what was going on, but he cried too, just because everyone else was. Everything felt so sad, I think even our house was weeping.

ERIC

On the day Dad left, Mom tried to stop him by throwing herself under the car so he couldn't back up or go forward. She kept saying, "You're going to have to run me over! You're not leaving!"

Dad yelled out the car window, "Come on Marie! Get out of there! Come on!"

It was awful. Dad pushed the car door open, grabbed Mom's legs and dragged her out from under the car. Mom started to punch him, and he shoved her onto the ground. Mom sank her head in her hands and started to cry.

Dad just drove away.

ERIC

Mom was screaming at the world again. She was in the yard in her blue-flowered dress, no shoes. Fists raised to a deaf and indifferent summer sky. A flood of profanity powered by her lungs filled the night. Our neighbor, Mr. Green, had heard it all before.

"Shut up Mrs. O'Reiley!"

Mom directed her barrage in his direction and the war of words was on again. Across the street, lights in the projects flicked on randomly. Faces filled the windows. The curious and nosy were up to watch the show.

I crouched inside the house with my hands over my ears, but it didn't help. I could still hear Mom's cursing. Suddenly, I just couldn't take it anymore. I had to get away. Quietly, I sneaked out the back door and ran across the street. I didn't want Mom to see me. She might have started screaming at me instead of Mr. Green. I found a bush to hide behind and peeked out as the police cars drove up. I was tempted to leave, but I stayed behind my bush and watched.

Three cops jumped out of the cars and approached Mom. She kept cursing, eyeing them as they come closer.

I couldn't believe what happened next. All three of the cops started knocking her down and punching her. I *knew* my mom was annoying, but three cops beating an unarmed woman was just too much! I clenched my fists in frustration. What should I do?

Then, one of the cops grabbed her from behind and wrapped his arm around her neck. He started punching her hard with his other fist.

I freaked out. That was *My mother* he was punching! I ran across the street, jumped on his back, and started trying to gouge his eyes out, choke him, hit him, anything I could do to make him stop beating my mother. The other cops dragged me off, handcuffed me, and stuffed me into the paddy wagon. A few minutes later, they threw my struggling and screaming mother in next to me.

So there I was. All I had wanted to do was get away from Mom and her screaming, and now I was sitting next to her in the paddy wagon, and she was still screaming and cursing her lungs out.

Suddenly, she stopped her swearing and looked at me with drunken comprehension

"Eric! You saved me! Oh Eric, you're such a good son, you made them stop beating me!" She gave me one of her huge, heart-warming smiles, reached over, and wrapped her arms around me.

Everything was all right again.

Once we got to the station, the police let me go home, but they threw Mom in the drunk tank.

Two days later Mom returned home, all battered black and blue.

ERIC

I was fourteen years old when my Mother was beaten by the cops. After being charged for disturbing the peace and resisting arrest, she came home with two black eyes and bruises all over her body. She immediately started a brutality lawsuit against the police department. The lawsuit dragged on for over two years, until I was 17.

On my 17th birthday, I had a car accident. It was a rainy, lazy day. I was hanging around with my friends Joey Walton and Pete Murphy drinking quarts of beer and quietly celebrating my birthday. We were trying to figure out how to spend the rest of the day, and, after much discussion, we decided to visit our friend Nancy Thompson. We arrived at to her apartment complex just as Nancy came rushing out the door. Her face lit up as she stopped in front of us and exclaimed, "What perfect timing! Can you guys move Greg's car for me?"

She explained that her parents didn't like Greg, and they would have his car towed if they saw it. It was parked in front of the building. She gave us the keys and told us to park it three blocks away. We said Suurreee!

This was a real birthday treat for me. None of us had our own cars, and my family didn't even have a car at all. Joey and Pete took their turns driving first. It turned out to be the longest three-block drive in the world. It was amazing how many "necessary" detours we took.

By the time it was my turn to drive I'd drunk yet another quart of beer. I had never driven before, and I was very nervous. To make matters worse, it had stopped raining and the streets were still wet. Four blocks. I just had to drive the car four blocks, and then we were going to park it. I started out in first, and that felt pretty good, so I decided to move into second, and that felt pretty good too. I was starting to feel a bit cocky (Yeessss, I can drive!*), when suddenly I saw a stop sign ahead. I slammed on my brakes. Well, you know what happens when you keep your foot on the brakes on a wet road! We slid about one hundred and fifty feet and hit a tree. My door flew open. I popped out of the car, skidded about thirty feet, and hit my head.*

I must have been wandering around in a daze, because I woke up about four or five blocks later and could feel blood pouring down my face, so I knew something was wrong. I figured the cops would come looking for me at home, and decided it was safer to go to my sister Amy's house.

When Amy opened her door, she took one look at me and ran to get some butterfly bandages for my head. I sat quietly while she patched me up. When I nearly passed out again, she told me to take a nap on her bed.

I was still resting about two hours later when there was a loud knock on the door. It was the cops. I hid beneath my nephew Evan's crib while Amy spoke with them. I could barely hear the conversation over the barking and growling of the police dogs. They must have followed my blood trail to the house.

"Do you have a search warrant?"

"No"

"Then you can't come into my house!"

"Well we know he's here!"

"If you don't have a search warrant, you can't come into this house!"

After going on this way for a while, the police finally left. I found out afterwards they had also been at Mom's house searching for me.

Two or three days later, when I got sick of hiding, I called the detective on the case and asked him if they were looking for me.

"We sure are!" he replied.

After some discussion, I agreed to go to the station to turn myself in. It turned out that Greg's parents claimed we had stolen the car, even though Nancy had given us the keys. I thought I was going to prison.

That was when my Mom struck her deal. She offered to drop her two-year-old brutality lawsuit against the city if they would let me sign up for the Navy instead of going to trial. The prosecutor agreed, as long as I passed the Navy's test. I passed, and that's how my Mom saved me from prison.

KATIE

The Florida room, our playroom, was furnished with only a TV sitting on a kitchen chair. It was built with concrete blocks on a concrete floor. My sister Amy told me Dad had added it on to the house for her thirteenth birthday party. Then he left. The room was his last little memento to us. We used to put our Christmas tree in there. Only after *Christmas of course, because we had to find one in the garbage first. There was no way we could afford to buy a tree.*

Sean, Colin, and I used to sit in front of the chair with a blanket over us and the TV, eating cereal. It was our sanctuary.

COLIN

One Saturday morning Sean, Katie, and I were in the Florida room under the blanket, eating cereal and watching cartoons. There was a knock on the door, and Sean ordered me to answer it. I peered out. Standing in front of me was a man with a bunch of plates in his hand.

"Is your mother home son?"

"Mom, there's a man at the door who wants to see you!"

I went back to the cartoons, but off to the side I could see Mom and the man talking.

"What do you want?" Mom demanded.

"Madame, if I could take a moment of your time, I'd like to show you a new design in dinnerware, made from durable, *shatterproof* plastic."

The salesman (What was a salesman doing in our neighborhood anyway?) tapped the plate against the concrete door frame.

"See how strong it is? And they come in lots of pretty colors!"

Mom had an intent look on her face. "Can I see them?"

"Sure!" The man handed the whole stack to Mom.

"They're light, too," he added with a satisfied look in his eyes.

Mom took the top plate off the stack, flipped it over a couple of times, and raised it over her head.

"Can it handle this?"

She slammed the plate onto the cement floor where it shattered into lots of pretty pink pieces. Then she decided to add a nice lime-green shatterless plate to the mess. The man grabbed for the rest of the plates as Mom let loose with another.

"Nope, this will never do," she said as she closed the door on the poor guy.

It was better than Mighty Mouse.

KATIE

"Hey, let's see if we can climb from the Banyan tree to the roof!" suggested Sean. Colin and I thought that sounded like a good adventure, so we agreed. Our house was only one story, so it didn't look too far from the ground, and the Banyan tree had a couple of large branches that almost overhung the roof. We started climbing the tree.

At first, it wasn't too scary. The tree had big thick branches that weren't very far apart. It was the perfect climbing tree. All three of us made it up fairly easily. Sean helped Colin and me on to a smaller branch that stretched out toward the house. Sean decided the easiest way to get from the branch to the roof was to go along the branch hand over hand until he was as close to the roof as possible. Then he would swing back and forth until his feet were directly over the roof and just drop safely down. The branch was about three feet above the flat roof of the house and about two feet back from it. Colin and I watched apprehensively as Sean tried out his plan. He swung his legs three times and then jumped. He made it!

Colin decided to go next. By now, I was having second thoughts about this whole enterprise, but I wasn't about to say anything to the boys. Colin didn't seem to be afraid, and he was younger than I was, so I didn't want to tell them I was scared. Colin slowly started to move along the branch. When he got to the end, he swung back and forth, back and forth.

"Just jump," yelled Sean, "I'll catch you!"

Colin jumped and landed safely in Sean's arms.

Now it was my turn. I looked nervously down. The ground seemed much farther away than it had when I'd been looking up at the tree. Oh well, if Colin could do it, so could I. I wiped my sweaty palms and started moving along the branch, keeping my eyes on Sean and Colin so I couldn't see the ground. I got to the end, and for a minute I was paralyzed with fear. The gap between the branch and the roof looked *enormous*.

"Come on!" called Colin. "You can do it!"

I started to swing, counting to three as I went. "One, Two, Three. . . ."

I flew through the air, but instead of landing in Sean's arms, I started to slide down the side of the house. Somehow, I managed to grab the edge of the roof. I frantically tried to get a toehold and boost myself up, but I just couldn't make it.

Sean looked down at me and called, "Hang on Katie! I'll get you my parachute!" A few minutes later he came back with a tiny plastic action figure that had a small parachute attached.

"Hold on to this when you fall, and you'll float to the ground," Sean suggested.

I reached up with one hand for the figure, and just as I grabbed it, I lost my hold on the roof and started to fall. Needless to say, the parachute didn't work.

My Mom was sewing in front of the window and happened to look up just as I flew past her. She screamed and ran out the door to see if I was hurt.

I must have had a guardian angel that day, because I didn't even have a scratch.

COLIN

Bored, bored, bored. What to do? Sean's with his friends, and Katie is at Betty's playing house or dolls or something. I'm bored. I'll play in the shed. I'll play hide and. . .no I can't do that. . .there's no one to play with. Bored. I could fold all those clothes. Nah. I wonder what would happen if I put soap powder in an ant hole? Neat! The ants are running around like crazy picking up and dropping pieces of soap powder. I wonder what they'd do with bleach? Wow, bleach smells strong. What does it taste like? GAG, GULP, SPUTTER, SPIT, GAG. Suddenly I don't feel so well. Oh oh, here comes Mom.

"What are you doing in there Colin?"

"I'm, ah, I'm folding clothes."

"Good for you. When you finish, clean the kitchen!"

"Mom, what would happen if I drank bleach?"

"YOU'D DIE!"

"Oh."

"Colin, where are you going? I thought you were folding clothes?"

"I. . .I. . .I 'gotta go!"

"Make sure you finish. . . ."

But I don't hear her 'cause I'm going to DIE!

Oh no! Oh no! I'm going to die! No more TV or Royal Castle or Sean beating me up or. . .and what if I go to HELL and burn forever? Is that a long time? And what about Katie, will she miss me? I wonder who'll come to my funeral? Will everyone cry? I'm gonna die!!!!

"COLIN, GET IN HERE!"

"What Mom?" I said with a sniffle.

"Have you been playing with the detergent?"

"I think so," I squeaked.

"I think so?" repeated Mom.

"I think I drank bleach."

"WHAT?!"

"I drank bleach and now I'm going to die!" I started crying.

"Come in here, quick." We ran into the kitchen and she mixed a big glass of mustard and milk.

"Hurry, drink this."

"Why?" I whined.

"So you won't die!"

GULP, GAG, GULP, BARF.

"Now take a bath and finish those clothes."

KATIE

Mom was crying again. Every night I could hear her crying and crying into her pillow. I covered my head so I couldn't hear her.

SEAN

One night I was lying in bed trying to go to sleep. It was just way too hot. I'd tried to cool off by taking a cold shower and lying on the bed soaking wet, but the water had already dried, and I was hot again. I lay and listened to Mom crying. It was the worst sound in the world and made me want to cry too. It seemed as if she did it every night, and that wasn't helping my sleeping problem.

Suddenly, the sound of her sobbing was broken by the crashing of glass. I could hear Mom yelling, "Get the fuck out of here you bastard."

I raced to Mom's room to see what was going on. Colin and Katie were right behind me. We ran into the back room where Mom was sleeping and watched in amazement as she leapt through the broken back window with a huge butcher knife in her hand. We could hear her yelling as she ran toward the front yard.

"You stay away from my house you hear me, you just stay away."

The three of us ran to the front window just in time to see Mom, propelled by fury, waving her butcher knife wildly over her head, chasing down the street after a fleeing would-be thief.

KATIE

Mom's favorite hangout was the First Street Pub. It was dark and dirty with a long scuffed up bar on one side and two old pool tables in the back. Fans turned slowly on the ceiling, but it always seemed hot and sweaty no matter what the weather. Mom would bring me in and set me on top of the bar while she ordered a drink. I'd sit and watch the people or pretend to read the writing scratched into the bar top. There was a jar of pickled eggs that stood next to the cash register. I never saw a single person eat one. I wondered what they tasted like, but didn't really want to find out.

Men would come up to Mom and flirt with her, but she never seemed to meet anyone she liked. She always dressed up when she went to the bar. She was a good seamstress and made herself pretty flowered dresses to wear. I think she was looking for a husband to help her take care of us, but so far she hadn't found one.

Then, one day everything was different. We had already been there two hours and Mom was pretty drunk. A loud smelly man came up and put his arm around her shoulder.

"Hey honey want to polish my belt buckle for me?" Mom blinked and then shoved his arm away.

"Leave me alone you greasy-haired bastard."

The man pulled Mom toward him and started to paw at her breast.

"You know you want it, so give it up to me sweetheart."

Suddenly, from behind them, a bottle crashed down on the man's head and he fell to the ground.

A large blurry-eyed stranger looked down at the smelly carcass and, weaving slightly, yelled, "The lady said to leave her alone."

Out of nowhere, someone jumped Mom's rescuer from behind and started to choke him.

Mom, never one to back off from a good fight, decided to rescue her rescuer and dragged the attacker off by his hair. Pretty soon the whole pub was in an uproar, Mom and her new hero were taking on all comers. I hid behind the bar and peeked out around the corner. Bodies were flying everywhere, but in the end, Mom and her friend had beaten everyone in the whole pub!

Mom started searching for me. "Katie, Katie, where are you? It's time to leave now."

I came out of hiding, and the three of us walked out the door together. I found out later that the man's name was Joe.

COLIN

And then one day Joe came to live with us. Mom had been getting desperate. One night she even woke Sean and me and told us to get down on our knees to pray that she wouldn't have to send us to foster homes. Mom just couldn't cope anymore. My dad wasn't giving her any child support, and she had no way of forcing him to help her. The rest of her family was as poor as we were and couldn't help either. I knew she had been going to bars to meet men, looking for a husband. That's where she met Joe.

Joe's moving in kept our family together. He was an alcoholic, but he was the only father figure I'd ever had. He even helped pay some of the bills.

One day Mom found a reason for all three of us to deserve a spanking. Maybe the house wasn't clean enough or maybe she was just in a mood. Anyway she said, "I'm fed up. All you three do is take, take, take. You never give." She turned to Joe. "You go belt them!"

Joe hesitated.

"If you don't, I will," Mom yelled.

Joe removed his belt and pointed to the door.

"Go into the bedroom."

Oh-oh, we're in trouble now. Sean, Katie and I went in and sat on the bed.

"Spank 'em good!" Mom yelled from the kitchen.

Joe stretched the belt in his hands and eyed us with a look of conspiracy. We sat with our hands in our laps, staring up at him in fear.

"I'm going to hit the bed and you scream," he whispered with his finger to his lips.

What?

He raised the belt over his head, and asked with a look if we understood. Sean nodded and Joe struck the bed. Sean screamed. Katie and I joined in.

And with that, we all had our little secret with Joe. I've always wondered if Mom had planned it that way.

SEAN

Joe and Mom had built a love nest in the shed behind our house. Complete with bed and TV, the nest was their hideaway from us. One evening I snuck in when they weren't around and found a half-empty bottle of vodka hidden under the bed. I'd never tried vodka before! I decided to take it. Then, wanting to share the booty, I rode my bike over to my friend Pete's house, and together we polished off the bottle.

I'd had beer before, but this was the first time I'd ever tried any hard liqueur. I couldn't believe how fast I got drunk! Riding my bike home was an enormous challenge. I kept falling off every ten feet. The bike had a mind of its own that night. I just couldn't get it to do what I said. Yelling at it to obey me didn't help–it just wasn't listening. Some of the younger kids in the neighborhood heard the racket I was making and started following me.

"Hey O'Reiley, what's the problem? Mamma never teach you to ride a bike?"

"Look at the dope! He can't even stay up for ten seconds!"

A cross-eyed, red-headed kid darted in front of me just as I managed to get back on and start riding again. I fell off. He danced around me laughing and pointing.

"Baby boy, can't ride a bike, nah nah, na nah nah, nah nah, na nah nah."

I finally made it home, vowing revenge on the red-headed kid the whole way. The next day I started searching for him. I didn't remember much about him except he had red hair and crossed eyes. That was enough. I found out he lived just down the block, but he was only eight years old and short for his age. I couldn't beat up a kid that young. It wouldn't be fair.

I decided to get Colin to do it. They were the same age and Colin was short too, so at least it would be a fair fight. I knew Colin would win–he was a tough little kid. He had to be with me as a brother. Besides, Colin had a bit of a crazy streak that helped him survive in our neighborhood, even with the disadvantage of his size. Best of all, Colin knew the secret to winning a fight–you can't care about getting hurt. Colin could give me my revenge.

COLIN

There was a cross-eyed, red-headed boy my age who moved into the projects. He was small like me, which was unusual. I was the smallest kid my age in the neighborhood. Anyhow, one day Sean ordered me to pick a fight with him, and of course I did. Not a major fist-to-face, draw-blood kind of fight. It was more like a wiggle and squirm on the ground and whoever ends on top wins kind of fight. The fight ended with me on top, so I went home feeling pretty good about myself and started bragging to Sean about my victory.

Suddenly I saw the kid's mom. She entered our yard with red hair ablaze, nostrils flared, and eyes askew.

"Mrs. O'Reiley!" she shrieked.

I hid in the closet.

"Mrs. O'Reiley!"

Mom, broom in hand, came in from the back room.

The lady was pounding on the door with each syllable of Mom's name: "Miss-is O-Reiley! Miss-is O-Reiley!"

"What's going on?" demanded Mom.

"Your son beat up Ricky."

"Who?"

"MY SON. He came home crying and said Colin beat him up."

I couldn't crawl any farther into the closet.

"So what?"

The lady started to open the louvered-glass door. Mom poked her with the broom.

Realizing that Mom was on my side, I emerged from the closet and joined Sean. He was watching with wide eyes and gaping mouth.

A tug of war ensued over the broom. Mom lost that one but managed to lock the door. It was a short-lived victory. The lady, with broom flailing and glass flying, proceeded to break the glass louvers, starting with the top one.

Mom told Sean, "Get the hose."

Meanwhile, Katie, along with the rest of the neighborhood, was across the street watching. For them it was an afternoon matinee–better than the soaps. Katie didn't think it was a good idea to come home yet.

Sean hauled the hose in through the back and handed the pinched end to Mom. Mom aimed the blast of water right in the middle of the lady's face, just as she was in mid swing on the last pane of glass.

It stopped her dead.

Mom opened the now-windowless door, grabbed a handful of sopping-wet red hair and tried to pull the lady into the house. For some reason, the lady didn't want to come in any more. Another tug of war followed.

Ricky's mother put up a good defense. Mom was only able to get her head into the doorway. Never one to miss a good opportunity, Mom started slamming the door on her head. Bam! Bam! Bam!

The lady, clearly the loser, finally got away and retreated for home.

Mom was really fired up then. I thought maybe she was going to turn on me for starting the whole thing, but no mention was made of my fight with Ricky. Instead, she turned to Katie who had just decided it was safe to come home.

"Why weren't you here helping your family?"

Katie didn't answer.

Mom slapped Katie across the face.

"Never stand by and just watch when your family needs help." She paused and thought for a moment. "Do you know where she lives?"

"Yes," Katie answered reluctantly.

"Good."

While Mom went into the back shed to plan her next move, we cleaned the house. Whenever Mom was "in a mood," we always cleaned the house. I never knew if it made a difference, but I wasn't one to risk testing it. It was one of those learned responses handed down from sibling to sibling. The house shone.

That night, Mom and Joe came in with the look of a plan in their eyes and the smell of spirits on their breath.

"Katie, show us where they live," demanded Mom.

KATIE

"Katie, show us where they live," demanded Mom.

I had to go. No one *ever* disobeyed my mother. So Mom, Joe, Sean, and I drove over to get revenge on the red-headed lady. It was nighttime and both Mom and Joe were drunk which was normal.

When we reached the red-headed lady's house, Mom and Joe got out of the car. Mom had a rock in each hand, and she started going around the house and breaking out all of the windows.

Sean and I hid in the car. I hate fights and arguing, and this was the last place I wanted to be.

Suddenly someone from inside the house yelled, "Mrs. O'Reiley we know that's you!"

Mom ignored them and kept going until all of the downstairs windows around the *entire* house were broken.

"That's for breaking our windows you bitch!" Mom yelled as she got back in the car. She turned to Sean.

"Now, where are your hiding places? I think Joe and I are going to need them tonight."

Sean thought for a moment and said, "Mom, you can hide under the house, and Joe. . . .I know! You can hide over by the church. There's a big bush there that's hollow inside and no one will see you."

Mom and Joe spent the rest of the night hiding while the cops looked for them. They were never caught.

SEAN

I hated going to church. Mom made us go every Sunday, but she and Joe never went. It didn't seem fair. Why did we have to go if they didn't? And we had to go 'cause she made us bring back the program to show her. The other thing I hated about church was the offering. I never had any money, so I would hit the bottom of the basket when it went by to make it sound as if I was putting money in. It was embarrassing.

I really didn't want to go that day because I didn't want to go to confession and have to tell about being drunk and getting Colin to beat up the red-headed kid. But there I was, stuck in church.

I thought about skipping confession, but I was worried about communion. You're not supposed to take communion until you confess.

I decided that no one would notice. I'd just go to communion anyway.

So, I walked to communion with Colin and Katie. We were at the front altar, and I was wondering if I would go to hell for this.

"SEAN O'REILEY!!!"

I jumped. The voice seemed to come out of nowhere. For a second I thought it was God.

"JUST WHAT DO YOU THINK YOU'RE DOING? YOU HAVE NOT CONFESSED YOUR SINS! YOU ARE NOT FIT TO TAKE COMMUNION. GO BACK TO YOUR PEW!" yelled the nun.

I could feel my face turning red. *That was it! I'd had it! I didn't want to go there in the first place, and I decided to never come back.*

I turned and walked out the door.

SEAN

"Sean, Katie, Colin, get in here right now!" Mom was yelling to us from the living room. We came slowly into the room. Mom was standing there with a belt. What had we done this time? With Mom, it could be anything, or it could be nothing.

"Kneel down on the floor, right now."

We kneeled. We always did what Mom said.

Suddenly, she started beating us with the belt. "I don't ever want you to kneel down for anybody, do you hear me? Don't you kneel down for *anybody*."

AMY

I was in my kitchen washing dishes when Mom started pounding on my window.

"Amy, Amy open up, you'll never believe what happened!"

I wiped my hands and went to the door. Mom came rushing in waving an envelope above her head. "Henry sent me a check for $600.00!"

I stared at her. "Dad? Dad sent you some money?"

"Yeah, can you believe it? Here, read the letter."

I took the note from her hand and glanced at it.

Dear Marie,

This is all the money I have, please hold on to it and use it sparingly."

Henry

"How did you get him to send you this?"

"I wrote him a letter and told him we were starving," she said excitedly. "Now I can finally buy the kids some clothes. I can enter Katie in that beauty contest. . . ."

"But Mom, don't you think you ought to use the money for food?"

She continued as if she didn't hear me. "I'm going to buy Katie that red velvet dress I've always wanted for her, and I can buy Colin that cute green velvet suit with a bow tie and he can wear it for Christmas. . . ."

"Mom, you don't have any food in the house, don't you think. . . ."

But she had already walked out the door.

A month later, Katie won the beauty contest. She really did look cute in her red velvet dress. The prize was a year's supply of ginger ale and a monkey.

The monkey ran away within a week.

KATIE

One day some city workers cut down the huge Banyan tree that was in front of our house. They left the stump standing. It was about six feet wide, five feet high, and had roots sticking out all over the place. Colin, Sean, and I took one look at it and decided it was the perfect place to build a cave! We started by digging a hole under the stump and then cutting some of the roots to make more room. About a foot down, we hit soft white sand that was really easy to dig.

We started going there every morning to dig some more. Our cave was *huge.* All three of us could sit inside it. The best part was that the entrance was camouflaged so no one could see us!

That gave Sean a great idea. He found some rotten tomatoes in the garbage and said, "Let's throw these at people and then hide in the cave!"

Colin and I both thought that sounded like fun. We hid ourselves behind the roots of the cave and waited for our first victim. Soon we saw Mrs. Peterson walking down the street with her poodle. Sean, Colin, and I threw our tomatoes at her and dove through the cave entrance.

Mrs. Peterson let out the loudest yell I've ever heard and came charging after us–but we'd disappeared! From inside our cave, we could hear her shouting

"Come out here you hooligans, come out right now."

Her dog was barking, she was yelling, and we just sat in our cave trying to hold in the laughter.

COLIN

One day Sean and his friend Dale decided to dig a long tunnel at the far end of our cave under the Banyan stump. They asked me to come along to help. After a couple of hours of hard work, we'd made a tunnel that was seven to eight feet long and about two feet in diameter. One end was closed and the other end opened into the cave. It was getting hot, so we decided it was time to quit for the day.

I should have known by the looks Sean and Dale gave each other that mischief was brewing, but I was too tired from the digging to pay much attention.

Sean turned to me and said, "Colin, go get the shovel. It's still back in the tunnel."

I didn't want to argue with Sean, so I obediently crawled in and grabbed the shovel. As I backed my way out, dragging the shovel with me, I started to smell smoke. Hurriedly, I twisted my body around. They'd built a fire in front of the tunnel!

I screamed and started choking on the smoke. Then I started trying to push sand on the fire with my feet, kicking at the flames and yelling at Sean and Dale to help me. It seemed to take forever, but I finally put the fire out. As I emerged from the tunnel, short of breath with my heart pounding, I saw them sitting in a corner laughing.

It's no wonder I'm claustrophobic.

SEAN

I was up late one night watching TV in the Florida room when Mom came walking in with a frozen look on her face.

"Mom what's wrong?"

She stared blankly at me and said, "The corned beef is on the stove."

"Mom, what are you talking about? The stove doesn't work."

"The corned beef is on the stove. I want you to get me some!"

I was getting a little nervous. "What corned beef? There's no corned beef!"

"Stop arguing and go get it!"

At this point I realized she was asleep. "Okay. . .okay, Mom. Whatever you say."

She started wandering through the house with me trailing behind her. This wasn't the first time she had gone sleepwalking, and I had a plan. I ran to the phone and called my friends Pete and Dale.

"You've got to get over here–she's walking again!"

By the time Pete and Dale arrived, Mom had wandered into the front yard, still asleep.

Pete yelled, "Hey Mrs. O'Reiley, what are you looking for?"

Mom turned blank eyes toward him and said, "Colin, where's Colin?"

I said, "Mom, he's over there, don't you see him?"

Mom looked toward the empty porch "Oh yeah, there he is. He's playing with Katie."

"Hey Mrs. O'Reiley, can you see the devil? He's coming right at you!"

Mom's eyes opened wide, and she screamed. Then she shook her head and looked wildly around. "What's going on, where am I?"

We all started laughing and ran away.

COLIN

"I should have gone to church that day." That's what Sean said, as if that were an excuse. It started off as a regular Sunday: wake early, find something for breakfast, and clean the house. Katie went to the Salvation Army church next door. Sean and I decided that he was having too much fun beating me up, so we stayed home. Oh, it wasn't the real bad stuff he was known for. It was just the basic pin me down, sit on my chest, and spit on me if I yelled kind of fun. I yelled. Yuck. Mom never seemed to hear this kind of yelling from the back room. She only came out when there was real pain inflicted, which there was that day.

I don't know where the padlock and chain came from, but all of a sudden it was dangling over my head as Sean said, "If you move again, I'll drop it."

This was not a small lock and chain but one of the heavy-duty kind. I moved. Sean let go. The lock alone would have been enough to hurt a lot, but this lock was towing a chain. It shattered my lower teeth upon impact.

"OOOOOOWWWWWWWW!"

Now Mom appeared.

"What's going on here?!"

"It was an accident," pleaded Sean.

At this point I was spitting out my teeth and worrying about how I was going to look without them.

"Colin, take a bath. Sean, go clean your room."

That was how Mom handled all crises–the offender had to clean and the injured party had to take a bath.

COLIN

Fixing my broken teeth became the terror of my life. We couldn't afford a regular dentist so Mom took me to a dental school downtown. These torture sessions went on for what seemed like years. I dreaded dentist days.

"Colin, hurry, we have to catch the bus!"

Sean and Katie were already getting ready to go to school. I wished I were going with them.

"Before you go, drink some of this Coke."

Mom took the half-full Coke bottle she was holding, spit into it, and swirled it around.

"Drink. It will protect you from evil."

"Oww, Mom!"

"Now!"

We drank from the bottle. No one in our family dared to talk back to Mom.

I was glad she was going with me to the dentist, but a trip on the bus with Mom was no picnic. When my face was dirty, she would spit on a corner of her dress and proceed to give me a bath. Yuck. If she passed wind, she'd elbow me and say, "Colin excuse yourself!"

This was very embarrassing stuff for a kid. And after all that, I still had the wannabe dentists to look forward to.

I had found a golf tee that I carried with me into "THE CHAIR." It had a nice sharp point I could squeeze into my palm when the pain was unbearable. I squeezed it a lot. I needed root canals on my three bottom teeth. The dental students had a real subject to work on, one who even screamed. I was the school guinea pig.

The first thing the students learn is how to give Novocain. One day I got eleven shots of it. Everyone had a turn to try.

I hate needles.

SEAN

I am not proud of some of the things I did when I was a kid, like scaring my Mom and smashing Colin's teeth. I was very frustrated because I felt as if the only thing I was good at was fighting. So of course I fought.

I'd play innocent and look as if I didn't know what I was doing so kids would come over to bully me. I hated bullies. I let them think they could pick on me, and then all of a sudden I'd be all over them. Before they knew what hit them, they'd be on the ground saying, "What the hell happened?"

Or I'd be at a dance and somebody would look at my girlfriend the wrong way and, boom, I'd punch him out. I was a great sucker puncher.

I think what I feel the worst about is how I used to torture Colin and Katie. You see I was frustrated because I couldn't read and they could. School always seemed so much easier for them than it was for me. Later I found out I was dyslexic, but at the time I just felt stupid. My teachers' perception of me was, "That guy is not going to make it." Year after year I heard, "You're not going to make it." So my opportunity at getting back at them was saying "Fuck you, watch." That's what motivated me. When I look back at those times, I find it sad that a negative thing was motivating me.

My career as a fighter really began in the second grade. The teacher would make me stand in a corner in front of the classroom every time I couldn't read something aloud. The rest of the kids in the class would make fun of me. I didn't like that. I solved the problem by meeting whichever kid had made fun of me after school, and having a talk with him about why it was inappropriate to laugh at me. Most kids didn't understand what I was trying to say, so I would have to physically demonstrate what would happen to them the next time they laughed at me. I was disciplined a lot at school for fighting.

My Mom never made me feel bad about things I wasn't good at–like reading. She helped me to feel good about the things I could *do. In fact, one day, she took advantage of my fighting skills and asked me to beat up the kid who lived next door in our duplex. He was constantly yelling at her and was basically rude and obnoxious whenever she was around. The next time he mouthed off to my Mom, I taught him a lesson in respect. He never bothered her again.*

KATIE

One day Mom came home with a rug and curtains she'd borrowed from somewhere. "Hurry! Katie, Sean, help me fix the living room."

We rushed around hanging the curtains, unrolling the rug, and cleaning the room until it was spotless. It looked real nice–not like our living room at all. Then there was a knock at the door. Mom and Sean looked at each other. Mom went to answer it while Sean went to get Joe.

Our school principal, Sean's teacher, and two other people I didn't know walked in. They all sat down with solemn expressions on their faces.

Finally the principal spoke. "Mrs. O'Reiley, we have a very serious problem here. We don't feel that young Sean is ready for the fourth grade. We've come here today to test him in front of you so that you understand why we want to keep him back a grade." Sean turned beet red. I'd never seen him look embarrassed before.

Mom immediately started defending Sean.

"What do you mean not ready for the fourth grade? Of course he's ready! Why if that stupid Johnson boy down the block. . . ."

"Mrs. O'Reiley," Sean's teacher interrupted, "The problem is that Sean doesn't know how to read."

"Of course Sean can read." Mom turned toward Sean, "You show them, honey. Read something for them."

Sean's teacher handed him a book. Sean just stood there staring at it, getting redder and redder. Finally he mumbled something and fled from the room.

Just then, Colin walked in. "Hey! We've got curtains! We've got a rug! Where'd they come from? Did we get rich?"

COLIN

"ALL RIGHT! LET'S GO! WE'RE GOING TO REDECORATE!!"

Mom had decided it was time to redecorate the house. Decorating the living room for Sean's reading interview had inspired her. I wasn't sure where the money was coming from, but I was ready to join in the fun. Mom said we were going to get new windows, new walls–the works. But first we had to tear down the old plaster. Take all of the plaster off the walls and ceiling so we could have new walls? We didn't ask questions. There must be a reason since Mom told us to, so we did it.

Sean invited our friend Dale to the house, gave him a hammer, and said, "Throw it at the wall!"

Dale looked at him as if he were crazy.

"Like this," Sean said. He took the hammer from Dale and flung it at the far wall. A big chunk of plaster cracked off and slid to the floor.

Dale couldn't believe it. Our friends had always thought our family was a little different, but who destroyed their own house?

I took the hammer next and tossed it against the ceiling. Plaster went flying.

Sean handed the hammer back to Dale and said, "Try it!"

Dale, looking unsure, threw it, and even more plaster came crashing down.

Word got around and all the neighborhood kids came over to help. Destruction is always fun. In no time at all, most of our walls and ceilings were down to studs and rafters with just the wood lath on them.

Mom never did get the money to redecorate.

KATIE

The winter after we removed the plaster from the walls and ceilings, Joe went to New York to help build the World's Fair. It was a hard winter. We had no electricity and no gas. The only thing we had was a barbecue grill in the house. Of course, we couldn't afford charcoal to cook with, so we burned the wood lath from the walls. It's a wonder we didn't get sick from the fumes. Every night was a barbecue night–it was like having a picnic that never ended.

When it was time to go to sleep, we would heat bricks on the grill and wrap them in cloth and paper. Then we'd put them under our mattress. Mom, Sean, Colin, and I would all sleep together to keep warm. We'd pile on all the blankets in the house. It was really cozy and Mom always made it fun. We'd tell each other ghost stories, sing songs, or just get into tickle fights. We never really noticed times were bad because we were having so much fun.

COLIN

Rats. I hated rats. Big ones and little ones–I hated them all.

Once the plaster was removed from the walls and ceilings, we could see them better. At night they ran across the bare rafters above us. The bed I shared with Sean had only one blanket with a huge hole in it. Guess who had the hole on his side? I peeked through the blanket and watched the parade of rats. They walked along the rafters on the way to the kitchen.

I'd silently beg, *Don't fall on me, please don't fall on me.*

SEAN

The house we lived in was a duplex. In order to pay the mortgage, we rented one side to a family of Cubans. Their side of the house had an outside electrical outlet. The electricity for that outlet went on their power bill. We ran an extension cord from the outlet into our side of the house so we could at least have lights. Other than that, we didn't have any electricity. Anyhow, one morning I found the cord unplugged, and when I went to plug it back in, Mrs. Rodriguez came out and yelled at me.

"You leave plug alone! Don't use plug! Don't use plug!"

I plugged it back in that night. They had a lot more money than we did so I figured they could afford it.

SEAN

The winter Joe was working at the World's Fair, Mom had no money. One day we ran out of the government-surplus food we got for free every month. All we'd had to eat the night before was noodles and cheese. There was no food for breakfast.

Mom called her friend, Mrs. Richards, for advice. After talking it over, they decided to shoplift. They wanted Katie and me to go along to help distract the sales clerks and to keep a lookout.

Shoplifting food took some planning. Both Mom and Mrs. Richards put on big puffy dresses. Mom made some drawstring bags on her sewing machine, and they tied them between their legs. Mrs. Richards put her baby in his stroller and loosened his diaper so she could hide food in it. She also had a little money, so they could buy some food while they were in the store and not look too suspicious.

Once we were in the store, Katie and I kept watch while Mom and Mrs. Richards started filling their bags with food. Mrs. Richards could walk with two canned hams between her legs and look normal! They stuffed food everywhere: in the drawstring bags, in Billy's diaper, in the stroller, in their bras–it was amazing! They went through the check-out line, paid for the groceries they were buying, and walked right out the door.

We pushed the shopping carts a few blocks away and then Mom and Mrs. Richards stopped to split the loot. I couldn't believe what they got: ham, cheese, bread, cookies, butter, carrots, cabbage, potatoes. . . .We loaded our share into the shopping cart and walked home.

I could hardly wait for dinner that night!

SEAN

One day Mom gave me ten dollars to buy myself a pair of shoes. I rode my bike over to my buddy Pete's house and we went together to the shoe store. It was a large place with very few salespeople. The shoes I liked were way back in a dark corner of the store. We looked around for help, but no one came. I guess the salesclerks figured that two young kids weren't actually going to buy anything. Then Pete had a brainstorm.

"Sean, I've got a great idea! Why don't you steal the shoes and keep the money? Just give your Mother some change; then we can go to the arcade and play pinball!"

I thought it sounded like a good idea so I agreed. We decided I would put on the new shoes, and we would leave my old shoes in their place. Then I would walk out the door wearing my new, stolen shoes.

The plan went off without a hitch and soon I was riding proudly home wearing my new shoes. Pete and I figured Mom should get six dollars and seventy-five cents in change, and I would keep three dollars and twenty-five cents. I didn't want to count it out in front of her, so I put her money in the pockets of my shorts. Then I tightly rolled the rest of the money and stuffed it into my sock. Pete and I rode to my house to give Mom her change.

As I was handing Mom the money, she glanced down to look at my new shoes and noticed the bulge made by the money.

"What do you have stuffed in your sock?"

My faithful buddy Pete decided now would be a good time to leave.

"Gotta go! See you Sean!" He ran out the door.

Mom turned back to me. "What's in your sock Sean?"

"Nothing."

"Don't tell me nothing! There's something in your sock and I want to see it."

Reluctantly, I unrolled the sock and showed her the money.

"Where did that come from?" Mom demanded. Then her eyes brightened in comprehension. "You stole those shoes, didn't you? Then you kept the money I gave you!"

I looked down at the ground and nodded my head. I tried to explain how no one at the store would help us, but Mom exploded. She grabbed me by the ear and started hauling me to the next room where she found a leather belt.

"Drop your pants."

Each lash with the belt was accompanied with Mom's voice yelling, "Thou shall not steal! Thou shall not steal! Thou shall not steal!" She kept beating me until I was crying uncontrollably.

"Now, we're going right down to that shoe store and you are going to give those shoes back."

I sniffled and shuffled my feet. "But. . .but. . .Mom. I've seen *you* steal. . .you and Mrs. Richards."

Mom glared at me. "Do you want another beating young man? We stole to feed our children when we didn't have any money. You stole for pleasure. That's two different things. You had the money to buy the shoes, and you chose to steal them instead. Now let's go! We're going to return those shoes."

COLIN

There was a toy gun that I wanted more than anything I could ever remember wanting before. I asked Mom if she could buy it for me but she said no. She didn't have money for toys. The gun was so cool. It was a cap gun and the caps exploded with a loud bang. I dreamt about that gun every night before I went to bed and, finally, I decided to do something about it.

The next day I walked casually to the store and sauntered in. I had a couple of cents so I went to the candy section and picked out some penny candies. Then, when no one was looking, I snatched the gun from the shelf and tucked it into my pants. Nervously, I paid for the candy and ran from the store.

I laughed and ran the whole way home, pointing and firing my gun at every living creature I saw. I was Buck Rogers, Daniel Boone, and Superman–all within five blocks. I kept on laughing and playing until. . .I ran smack into Mom. She stopped walking and turned the full blast of her piercing blue eyes on me.

"Where'd you get that gun?"

I looked down at my shoes.

"I bought it."

"And where did you get the money to buy it?"

I decided that I should look her in the eyes while I lied. Maybe then she'd believe me. I looked up.

"I mowed a guy's lawn and he gave me three dollars."

"Where was this lawn?"

"Over on Seventy-fifth Street."

"Well we're going over there right now, and you're going to show me the lawn!"

Now I was in trouble. She and I started walking toward Seventy-Fifth Street. I figured I could find a lawn that looked newly mowed, and tell her that I had mowed it. I started looking back and forth.

"There it is!" I said in relief. I pointed to a freshly mowed lawn. Mom looked down at me.

"This is the lawn?"

"Yeah, that's the lawn I mowed."

"You're sure?"

"That's the lawn," I said confidently.

Mom proceeded to walk to the front door.

"What are you doing?" I yelled in alarm.

Mom rang the doorbell and a man looked out. I could see her asking him a question and pointing toward me on the sidewalk. The man shook his head and closed the door. Mom came striding back toward me, her face red and furious.

"WHERE DID YOU GET THAT GUN?"

"I. . .I stole it." My face crumpled and I started crying. Mom grabbed me by the arm and started hauling me down the street.

"I don't ever want to catch you stealing again, do you hear me? If I ever catch you stealing again, you're going to get a beating so bad you won't be able to sit down for a month," she yelled as she yanked my arm. "Now we're going right down to that store. You're going to return that gun, and you're going to apologize to the manager for what you did! Do you hear me?"

I nodded glumly.

Returning that gun was the most embarrassing moment of my life. My Mom tried so hard to teach us proper values, but she had a rough time making them stick considering how and where we were growing up.

SEAN

Our Thanksgiving Basket
(To feed four people)

2 Cornish Game Hens
4 Potatoes
1 Can of Corn
1 Can of Peaches
1 Loaf of Bread

Happy Thanksgiving from the Ladies of the Local Church!

I decided to supplement our Thanksgiving dinner by stealing money from the poor box at church. I figured the poor box was for poor people and, since I was poor, that meant it was for me. I was just saving the church the trouble of finding me and bringing me the money. Besides, the church was getting remodeled, so I figured they must be raking in the dough.

I took a piece of bubble gum and stuck it on the end of a pencil. Then I snuck into the church and crept to the poor box. The slit in the top of the box was just big enough to stick the pencil through. I pulled out the money coin by coin.

I gave the money to Mom and told her I had found it on the street.

COLIN

I Hate Christmas, I Hate Christmas, I Hate Christmas.
I Hate Christmas, I Hate Christmas, I Hate Christmas.
I Hate Christmas, I Hate Christmas, I Hate Christmas.
I Hate Christmas, I Hate Christmas, I Hate Christmas.
I Hate Christmas, I Hate Christmas, I Hate Christmas.
I Hate Christmas, I Hate Christmas, I Hate Christmas.
I Hate Christmas, I Hate Christmas, I Hate Christmas.
I Hate Christmas, I Hate Christmas, I Hate Christmas.
I Hate Christmas, I Hate Christmas, I Hate Christmas.
I Hate Christmas, I Hate Christmas, I Hate Christmas.
I Hate Christmas, I Hate Christmas, I Hate Christmas.
I Hate Christmas, I Hate Christmas, I Hate Christmas.
I Hate Christmas, I Hate Christmas, I Hate Christmas.
I Hate Christmas, I Hate Christmas, I Hate Christmas.
I Hate Christmas, I Hate Christmas, I Hate Christmas.
I Hate Christmas, I Hate Christmas, I Hate Christmas.
I Hate Christmas, I Hate Christmas, I Hate Christmas.
I Hate Christmas, I Hate Christmas, I Hate Christmas.

KATIE

One year Mom decided we would have our own Christmas tree–not one that we got out of someone else's garbage after Christmas was over. She decided to cut down the tree in our front yard. She also bought a package of tinsel and we put it all over the tree. It looked really pretty.

Colin, Sean, and I wrapped all the empty boxes and books we could find and put them under the tree. We used newspaper, some old wrapping paper we found in the neighbor's garbage, and paper that we drew pictures on. It looked as if we had lots of presents! I could hardly wait for our friends to come over. They would think we were rich!

COLIN

I was scared of our bathroom. I usually tried not to go there at night, but one night I woke and just *had* to go. I tried to shake Sean awake.

"Sean, wake up! Come to the bathroom with me."

He just grumbled and turned over.

I tried again. "Sean! Sean, wake up."

Next thing I knew, he lashed out and almost punched me in the jaw.

"Leave me *alone*!"

I had no choice so I crept out of bed and started down the hall with my flashlight.

The house was really spooky at night. There were strange rustling noises, and I could hear a number of rats squeaking and fighting somewhere nearby. Suddenly I saw two beady red eyes glowing at me from an open closet. I leapt back and stifled a yell. It was a *huge* rat that was caught in one of our traps. The rat had tried to drag itself, trap and all, out of the closet, but Sean had tied a rope onto the trap and had tied the other end to a nail. The rat had exhausted itself trying to pull away. Now it just sat there staring at me.

Once I stopped shaking, I slowly backed away from the staring rat and opened the bathroom door. The floor was missing so I had to walk carefully on the floor joists to get to the toilet.

I looked up at the evil trap door in the ceiling. Sure enough, it was open. No matter how many times I closed it somehow it just kept opening again. Who lived up there? My older brother, John, had once told me that someone was always watching me–even when I was alone in the bathroom. Now I realize that he meant God, but back then I thought that someone lived in our attic and peeked at us through the trap door. I didn't take my eyes off the trap door.

When I finally glanced down, I realized the toilet lid was still down and I had peed all over it! I panicked. What would Mom say?

Then I heard a scratching noise at the window and saw a skeleton looking in at me! I pulled up my pants, ran down the hall, jumped in my bed, and pulled the blanket over my head. From then on, I peed in my bedroom closet at night!

KATIE

My oldest brother Daniel was on leave from the Navy so he and Amy decided to throw a big party. Mom and Joe went to the First Street Pub and Colin, Sean, and I went to bed. I was having a hard time sleeping. People were dancing and yelling. It sounded as if they were all drunk.

As I lay in bed trying to doze off, I heard the door to my room quietly open. A dark figure crept in. I closed my eyes and pretended I was asleep. My heart was pounding so hard that I thought the intruder would hear it. The figure moved closer and I could feel his weight as he sat on the bed. I felt the covers move and slowly a hand slid over my arm and started to stroke my breast. I closed my eyes tighter as the hand crept lower and started fondling me between my legs. My mind froze in horror and I didn't know what to do. Then I had an idea. I shifted slightly and said in as sleepy, whiny a voice as I could manage, "I'm t h i r s t y. . . ."

"I'll get you something to drink," he whispered.

I recognized the voice. It was Bob, my brother Daniel's friend. As soon as he left the room, I opened my eyes, jumped out of bed, and ran as fast as I could to find Amy. My body started shaking and my teeth were chattering as I blurted out what had happened.

Amy started cursing, "That bastard, that little bastard," as she ran to find Daniel. When Daniel heard the story he stormed through the house looking for Bob.

"YOU SICK SON OF A BITCH! GET OUT OF OUR HOUSE." Daniel grabbed Bob, threw him against the wall, and started punching him. Bob tried to run outside, but Daniel caught him in a choke hold and yelled in his ear.

"DON'T YOU EVER COME BACK HERE! IF I SEE YOUR FACE AGAIN, I'LL KILL YOU! YOU GODDAMN PERVERT!" Bob ran, face bleeding, from the house.

KATIE

Jenny Jones from down the street always had great birthday parties–much more fun for kids than Amy and Daniel's parties! She had cake, and games, and bikes to ride, and ice cream, and lots of other kids to play with, and a clown, and party hats, and prizes, and. . . Well for some reason Mom didn't want us to go to Jenny's party. I think she thought Jenny's parents spoiled her. Or maybe Mom was afraid we'd want that kind of birthday party too, and then she'd have to say no since we couldn't afford it. Colin, Sean, and I didn't care what her reason was. We just wanted to go and have a good time.

On the day of Jenny's party, Mom and Joe were in the shed in back of the house watching TV and drinking vodka. We stuck our heads through the open doorway and told them we were going to play in the cave under the Banyan tree. Mom gave us a blurry nod and turned back to the TV. Joe didn't even notice we were there. We figured it was safe to leave since they seemed pretty out of it. So after hanging out by the cave for a few minutes, we took off for the party.

It was great! It was everything we had dreamed of. There was lemon cake with chocolate frosting, chocolate ice cream, and everyone got a little bag with candy and a noise maker in it!

Colin and I decided to take turns riding Jenny's bike up and down the block. Colin was on the handlebars and I was pedaling. I had to concentrate very hard to keep the bike going in a straight line.

Suddenly one of the kids from the party came running toward us yelling, "KATIE! YOUR MOM'S LOOKING FOR YOU AT JENNY'S HOUSE!!"

All I could think of was, *Oh no! She's drunk and she's at the party! I've got to get out of here!* I panicked and jumped off the bike, forgetting about Colin on the handlebars.

Colin started yelling as the bike kept moving forward without me. It crashed into a bush.

I rushed over, grabbed Colin, and brushed him off. Then we both started running as fast as we could, leaving the bike where it had fallen.

"Let's go through the courts! She won't look for us that way," Colin suggested.

I breathlessly agreed and we ran in that direction.

Sean appeared from around the corner of a house. He must have had the same idea.

"Did she see you?" he asked me.

"No, I think we got away."

"Me too!" he replied.

But Mom was smarter than we thought. She must have figured we'd come home the back way. She appeared out of nowhere.

"I told you kids not to go to that party! Now come home right now!" She grabbed a hunk of my hair and started pulling me toward the house. (The boys had crew cuts so she couldn't grab their hair.) I yelled the whole way home.

Still, it was a *great* party!

COLIN

Katie and I were watching TV in the Florida room when we heard the mailman drop a letter through the slot in the front door. Mom went to get it and slit it open.

"OH MY GOD! OH MY GOD! OH MY GOD! HE'S DEAD!"

Katie and I ran to Mom.

"What's wrong? Who's dead?" we yelled.

"ERIC! ERIC! OH GOD, NO!"

"Eric's dead? Eric can't be dead." Katie started to cry.

Mom sank to the floor crying and wailing. I grabbed the letter from her hand. It was from Eric.

"Mom, Eric's not dead. He wrote this letter. How can he be dead?"

"He's dead! He's dead! Look at this picture." She handed me a photo she'd been clutching.

"But Mom, he's in the picture! How can he be dead?"

"His head is cut off! They cut his head off!"

I looked closer at the photo and noticed the top of Eric's head was cropped out. I put my arms around Mom.

"It's just a picture. They didn't cut his head off. Really, it's just a picture. Eric's alive. Please stop crying, Mom. Please."

Dear President Kennedy,

Today I saw Jesus walking down the street with a hammer, and I thought I should write to tell you that I think it is your job to "hammer out love between the brothers and sisters all over this land." President Kennedy, I think you are the man to do the job. You should start with my ex-husband who is off in the Caribbean with his new wife while I'm here starving with three of our seven children. Hammer on him for me. But you should be careful. Jesus is a martyr and you are close to his age when he died, and I think you are a Jesus of the world come to save people, but of course you are not Jesus. That would be blasphemy. But you understand–you're Catholic too. Can you believe it? The Church wouldn't cash the check my sister gave me. My sister's a *nun*, the check was from a convent, and they wouldn't cash it and my children are hungry. I'm never going to that church again. Maybe you can hammer on that church for me while you're at it.

I hope to see you soon Mr. President.

Yours truly,

Marie O'Reiley

SEAN

I was sitting in the kitchen eating cereal at the picnic table when I heard a knocking on the front door. I went to answer it. Standing on the stoop were two men in dark suits and ties. No one dressed like that in our neighborhood so I knew something was wrong. Or perhaps we'd won one of those contests Mom kept entering.

"Is your mother home, son?"

(I decided they must be bill collectors.) "No, she's out."

"Do you know when she'll be back in?"

"Nope."

Suddenly Mom was behind me. "Sean, who's there?"

"Madam, we're from the secret service and we'd like to ask you a few questions."

Mom didn't invite them in. She crossed her arms. "Well go ahead and ask."

"Madam, did you recently write a letter to President Kennedy?"

"What's it to you?"

"Madam, your letter seemed to threaten the president. Can you tell us what you meant by it?"

"Threaten the president? What! Are you people crazy? I never threatened the president! Why would I threaten the president? He's a hero. I love the President. I can't believe you thought I was threatening him! Can't you fools read?" Her voice got louder and louder. "Get off of my property you stupid idiots! Get off right now! I don't believe you're from the Secret

Service! President Kennedy knows I wouldn't threaten him, I'm going to call the police. . . ."

They left. Most people did when Mom started on one of her rampages.

KATIE

I was in school the day President Kennedy was shot. When they announced it over the PA system, all I could think about was how Mom would react. President Kennedy was her idol. He was an Irish Catholic man who was not only successful but was also the leader of our country. Kennedy's life gave her hope.

When we got home from school, Mom was rummaging through a drawer in the kitchen where she kept things that had special meaning only to her. She had tears streaming from her eyes and she was muttering, "Why oh Lord? Why did you take him? He was so young. Oh Lord, I don't understand."

Then she took out a hammer from the drawer and started singing over and over, "If I had a hammer. . .I'd hammer in the morning. . .If I had a hammer. . . ."

Colin and I backed away from her and went to the Florida room to watch TV. Every channel had coverage of Kennedy's death. Mom heard it and came in to watch with us. She was sobbing as if she'd never stop. Finally, she cried herself to sleep.

KATIE

Oh no. . .mom's having one of her attacks again. . . .maybe if i do what she says and pray to the cross she'll stop yelling. . .why isn't amy here?. . .where did she go?. . .why did she leave us?. . .mom's making us sing "if i had a hammer" again. . . "if i had a hammer, i'd hammer in the morning, i'd hammer. . ."i hate this song. . .i'm scared of mom when she gets this way. . .oh no, colin and sean are gone too. . .where is everyone?. . .mom wants me to go outside and go into the cave with her. . .i don't want to go. . . .how's she going to fit in the cave anyhow?. . .there's amy. . .she's on the corner. . .she'll make sure I'm okay. . .mom actually fits in the cave. . .i can't believe she's here. . .what does she want anyway?. . .i'll go out the back exit. . .why did she pull me back?. . .what does she want?. . .how can i get out?. . .i know. . .i'll tell her she doesn't have her hammer. . .maybe if i remind her of it she'll let me go get it. . .yeah, that's it. . .she needs the hammer for her ritual. . .i'll get it, she trusts me to get it for her. . .finally i'm out. . .amy's called the police. . .they are waiting outside the cave. . .mom won't come out. . .at least the police are being nice to her this time. . .she's coming out for her hammer. . . .the police are taking mom to the hospital. . . .i'm so glad i'm out of the cave.

AMY

I had stopped at the house to drop off some soup on my way to work. Mom was acting really strange. She kept mumbling to herself that Kennedy was dead and the devil was coming. Then she wanted Sean, Colin, and Katie to get down on their knees, pray to the cross on the wall, and sing "If I Had a Hammer." While they were doing this, she ran to a drawer in the kitchen, pulled out a hammer and carefully placed it under the cross. Most of what she said made no sense at all. When she tried to get me to kneel with the kids, I told her I had to go to work, but I'd be right back. She didn't really notice when I left, but as I glanced behind me, I saw Katie throw me a look of pure panic.

I ran as fast as I could to the nearest neighbor's house with a phone and called the police.

"Please help us! I need someone to take my Mother to the hospital! She's acting really crazy and she needs help! But, please, please, please, she doesn't like the police; be nice to her. She's just sick, not a criminal."

I told them where she lived and ran back to the house. Once I was there, I waited for the police from a corner where I could watch the house. In a minute, Mom and Katie came out of the front door and started walking toward the cave. Mom pushed Katie in and followed after her. I didn't believe Mom could actually fit inside.

Just then a police car arrived. I explained what was going on and pleaded with them to be nice to her. We had started walking across the street when Katie climbed out of the cave. She ran over to me crying. I held her while a policeman started talking to Mom from the cave entrance. He motioned me over.

"See if you can talk her out of there."

I was scared Mom would start cursing at the cops and they would beat her like before.

"Please Mom. Come out. No one's going to hurt you. Please Mom. . .it's okay. We're going to take you to the hospital so you can get a nice long rest. Please, please come out."

Finally, after about half an hour, she emerged calmly from the cave and walked to the police car with me. She sat in the back seat and I sat in the front.

"Shirley, Shirley, where are we going?"

"Mom, it's Amy."

"No, you're Shirley Temple and we're going to the zoo, the zoo, who are you, going to the zoo. If I had a hammer, I'd hammer in the morning, I'd bam her in the evening. Did you know the devil's coming? We have to pray right now to stop him. Devil's coming, Shirley. Shirley, Shirley?"

"Yes Mom?"

"Shirley, where are we going?"

After what seemed like the longest drive in the world, we got to the sanitarium. A nurse handed me some forms to fill out.

"And what's your last name Shirley?"

"My name is not Shirley."

"But your Mother keeps calling you Shirley."

"Well, why do you think I'm checking her in here? She's acting crazy. My name is Amy."

Mom piped in, "I will not tell my name in vain . . . . I will not tell my name in vain . . . . I will not tell my name in vain . . . ."

Once I'd gotten Mom checked in, all I wanted to do was sit down and cry. Then I remembered the kids. Who would take care of them? I decided to call my grandma Nana for help.

SEAN

Katie was mad at Colin and me when we ran away and left her alone to go into the cave with Mom. No way was I going in that cave–I knew when my Mom was nuts. But I did go to visit Mom in the sanitarium. It was an old converted mansion that reminded me of a haunted house. We could hear the people inside screaming as we walked through the front door. Katie and Colin were too young to visit and had to sit downstairs, but I was allowed to see Mom.

I was led down a dark narrow hallway with hardwood floors. Each door had a wire mesh on it and I could hear the people inside moaning and mumbling to themselves. A woman with lipstick all over her face stopped in front of me and gave me a big hug.

"Robert, it's good to see you again!" Then she whispered, "Are you a virgin? We're all nuns here."

That was where my Mother was taken, to a place full of crazies. When I saw her, her eyes looked dull from the drugs they'd given her. She said they'd given her shock treatment.

"But it ain't working–you can't make a scrambled egg out of a hard-boiled egg. Never 'gonna work. . . ."

She begged me to help her get out. "Sean, these people are crazy! You 'gotta get me out of here!"

I wished I could. I was getting sick of Nana's cooking.

KATIE

I hated having Nana stay with us. She told us Mom was never going to get better and that she'd have to stay with us forever. Amy said that wasn't true and Mom would get better soon. I hoped so. I hated Nana's cooking.

Sean sat next to the garbage can at dinner and wouldn't let us throw away any of Nana's food–no matter how bad it was. He threw *his* food away and made Colin and I eat ours. Sometimes I hated Sean too. But I hated Nana more. She killed our pet duck and made us eat it. Our poor duck. We had made a cool lake for it by digging a hole in the backyard and putting a washtub in it. Why did Nana have to kill it? Nana never liked our duck, but that didn't mean she had to make us eat it.

COLIN

A Day in the Life of Nana's Towel

Dry face and hands in the morning. Rest on shoulder. Wipe out frying pan after government surplus meat and egg breakfast. Wipe egg and goo off my face. Hang from shoulder. Clean off table. Dry dishes. With a flick of a wrist–faster than Quick Draw McGraw–hit a cockroach crawling up the wall. Back on shoulder.

I shudder to think of what other duties the towel was used for during the day. By evening it was getting a little stiff, but it was still good enough to wipe the day's dirt off my face. *Rest on shoulder. Wipe table for dinner. Dry dinner dishes.* Now where do you think the towel spent the night? In the laundry? No, at night the towel had special duties. If there were leftovers (which there usually were when Nana cooked her specialty–spam spaghetti) the towel would be under her bed. It covered the leftovers so we wouldn't steal them. Or perhaps it was so the millions of cockroaches in our house wouldn't get to them.

KATIE

Eric was on leave from the Navy so he and I decided to visit Mom at the hospital. Mom had been there about two months already. They'd moved her to a less restricted ward, and this was the first time I'd been allowed to visit her. I missed her so much and was really excited to see her.

We walked through the long narrow hallway to Mom's ward and asked for her at the front desk. A few minutes later a nurse came out and spoke to Eric.

"We're having a little trouble finding your Mother, but don't worry, we'll locate her."

Eric stared at the nurse. "A little trouble finding her? What the hell are you talking about? Don't you keep track of your patients here?"

We watched nervously as the nurses and orderlies frantically ran around opening and closing doors searching for Mom.

I was starting to get scared. What had happened to her?

Then Mom's doctor walked toward us. "Don't worry, we'll find her. We'll find her. She's got to be here somewhere."

Eric said, "This is ridiculous, let me use the phone."

He called our house and spoke with Sean. "You'll never believe what's going on here! They've lost Mom!" Suddenly he yelled, "What do you mean she's with you? How did she get out?"

It turned out that the week before, during Amy's last visit, Mom had asked her for a quarter. Once Mom was allowed to use the elevators, she just went downstairs and used the quarter Amy had given her to call a cab from the pay phone on the first floor. When the taxi arrived, she walked right out the door and told the driver to take her home.

The doctor said to Eric, "Try to get your Mom to come back."

Eric figured that since Mom was smart enough to escape from the hospital, he wasn't going to force her back unless she wanted to go. We were all happy Mom was finally home.

SEAN

I was walking through a long, dark, narrow hallway towards a bright, pulsing red light. On either side of me were doors with mesh windows. Suddenly a hand reached through the mesh and grabbed me. I screamed and hit it away. A moaning filled the air. I walked closer and closer to the pulsing light. It surrounded a door in front of me.

I tried to open the door, but it was locked. I started to pound on it again and again, yelling, "Let me in! Let me in!"

The moaning got louder.

Then the door swung open, but the light had gone out. I walked in and searched for a light switch. I found one and flipped it on. The door slammed shut behind me. In front of me was a giant cockroach and the floor was covered with millions and millions of little roaches. They started coming toward me faster and faster. I started screaming but no one answered. I tried the door but it was locked. The roaches had reached me . . . . They were crawling all over me . . . . I started jumping around screaming and throwing them off.

Then I woke–only to find that my dream was real and I had roaches crawling all over me.

KATIE

Amy and her husband, Stuart, got into a fight and Amy came back home to live with us. Mom was really happy about it. She didn't like the way Stuart treated Amy. I liked it when Amy visited so I was happy too. But one morning Amy said she was moving out and going back to Stuart. She and Mom got into a huge argument about it. They were yelling and screaming all over the house. It ended when Amy loaded her car and drove off, saying she'd be back in the afternoon for the rest of her stuff. Mom called Sean, Colin, and I into the kitchen.

"Kids, here's three dollars. Take it and go to the Penny Arcade." Mom and Joe usually sent us to the Penny Arcade when they wanted to get really drunk and didn't want us around.

We shouted, "Thanks Mom!" and ran off before she could change her mind. We spent the next couple of hours at the arcade and then walked home. As we got closer to our house, we noticed a nasty, smoky smell.

Sean pointed ahead. "Hey look at that! There's a fire in our front yard!" We got there just as Amy and Stuart started pouring water on the fire with the garden hose.

"What happened? What is it?" we shouted.

"Mom and Joe put all my stuff outside, poured gasoline on it, and set it on fire," Amy said sadly. "I guess they're mad at me for moving back with Stuart."

Stuart started cursing. “I’ve had enough of your God-damn, crazy family.” He stomped off toward the back of the house where the shed was.

Amy, Sean, Colin, and I followed close behind.

Stuart reached the shed and started yelling. “Come on out! I’m sick of you people interfering in my marriage! Get out of there! Come on out you cowards!”

Joe appeared in the doorway and stood there weaving drunkenly, opening and closing his fists.

“Get off of my property!” He shouted, “Get off and don’t come back!”

“*Your* property! That’s a laugh! You don’t own nothing, old man! You’re nothing but an old drunken fool!”

Joe gave a bellow of rage and started running at Stuart. Suddenly Stuart whipped out a gun from his jacket and shot at Joe. The bullet missed Joe and went through the shed door, smashing the TV inside. Pandemonium followed.

Sean, Colin, and I took one look at the gun, panicked, and ran into the house screaming. Even though there were only three of us, there seemed to be kids everywhere–kids screaming and yelling and trying to find a place to hide. While we were frantically diving for cover, Amy grabbed the gun from Stuart.

“STOP IT YOU FOOL! WHAT ARE YOU DOING?”

Stuart stopped in his tracks and stared stupidly at the gun.

Just then, a police car arrived. One of the neighbors must have called earlier because of the fire and the yelling. Stuart was arrested.

Amy left with him. As she later said, “Love is blind.”

COLIN

Dear Mr. Preasident

After you become Preasident for the second time could you put aside a day for Kids Day to remember John F. Kenndy by? If you could, make it in the summer time on a Saterday so everybody could be together. Maybe everyone could have a Barbaqu because it doesn't cost much. We use to have a barbaqu every night because our lights were out.

I'm in the six grade and 11 years old. I have four brothers and two sisters. My brother was a drop out and he went in the Navey. He studied hard to go to colledge.

I hope it is not to cold up there when you become preasident again.

Yours truly,
Colin O'Reiley

P.S. My Mom made me write this.
P.P.S. She's really sad that Preasident Kenndy died. So am I.

KATIE

In my class there was a kid, Roberto, who was always bothering me. He never left me alone at recess. One time he tripped me when I ran out the door and yelled, "I see London, I see France, I see Katie's underpants!" I hated him. Once, on the last day of school, he sprayed ink from a water gun all over my dress and ruined it. My Mom had made the dress and it was my favorite. When Sean saw what Roberto had done, he swore he'd get even and make Roberto stop bothering me. I forgot all about it over the summer, but Sean didn't forget.

On the first day of school, Sean cut his classes and came to my school. He waited until we were outside in PE class, picked up a two-by-four, and hit Roberto across the back. "You leave my sister alone you bastard, or I'll hurt you even worse!"

The teacher came running over and ordered Sean to leave. I was taken to the principal's office. The principal gave me a note to give to Mom and asked for a reply. I wished he hadn't done that. Mom always wrote crazy letters to my teachers. It was embarrassing. I tried not delivering them, but Mom always asked for an answer.

This letter was no exception:

Dear Mr. Wallace,

My son Sean is the avenger. If you had to sew your own kids' clothes because you had no money, you'd know what I mean. Since Kennedy died, no one understands these things. Maybe his ghost will explain them to you. Leave Sean alone since you so obviously are a moron. He's worth ten of you. And stop harassing my Katie. She deserves a better principal. I think I'll talk to Kennedy about that.

Sincerely yours,

Marie O'Reiley

Sean

One Saturday some friends and I were going to the movie theater when we saw a group of people gathered around two kids who were fighting. We pushed our way to the front of the excited crowd to see who it was, and there was my little brother Colin getting clobbered by some kid who was a lot bigger than he was. (Colin was small for his age.) I saw red. *Nobody* was allowed to pick on my brother. But then I realized something. I wasn't always going to be there to protect Colin. He was old enough now that he should start learning to protect himself. So instead of pulling the guy off him, I went over to them, stuck my face up to Colin's, and yelled, "If you don't win this fight, I'm going to kick your ass myself!"

Colin started crying but he kept right on fighting–all the way to victory.

COLIN

"Colin, come here! Quick!" Mom gestured me over to her. I had been playing outside with our friends Dale and Pete when she called me aside.

"Sean's alone in the other side of the house with a girl," Mom whispered. One side of our duplex was empty while we looked for new renters. It was the perfect place for a romantic rendezvous. "I want you and your friends to interrupt them," she continued urgently. "I don't want Sean getting himself or some girl in trouble."

I gave Mom a huge mischievous grin. "Whatever you say!" I replied happily. Then I ran over to Dale and Pete and explained the situation. They were eager to help out. We figured if we were lucky we might even get to see a naked girl! Very quietly the three of us snuck around to the back of the duplex and slowly let ourselves in. We carefully shut the door so it wouldn't squeak and crept toward the back bedroom where there were muffled noises coming through the wall.

Giggling softly, we listened at the bedroom door for a moment. It sure sounded as if something interesting were going on. Then we burst into the room, hoping to catch them in "The Act." The girl let out a loud scream as the door slammed open. Sean started cursing and leapt off the mattress where they'd been lying. Unfortunately for us, both Sean and the girl had their clothes on. However, we knew they'd been doing *something,* so the three of us started our taunting.

"Caught you! Caught you!"

"What have you been doing old Seany boy?"

"Did you get lucky today Seany?"

Sean turned bright red. "Get out of here!" he yelled, "before I kill the lot of you."

We ran out the door laughing.

Mission Accomplished.

SEAN

Like most fifteen-year-old boys, I was obsessed with sex. My biggest fear was that I was going to be an adult and still a virgin. It seemed as if every time I'd get a girl alone, Colin and his friends would interrupt me. The situation was getting desperate. I even had someone read my Tarot cards to find out when I would lose my virginity. The cards said it wouldn't happen until I was 18.

But I had a plan. I waited for an evening when Colin and Katie were spending the night at Amy's house. Then, when Mom and Joe were asleep, I snuck my main girlfriend, Rachel, into the house. This time I wanted to try it in a ***real*** *bed. Holding hands, I led Rachel into my bedroom. We started to kiss. This was it! I was finally going to do it! We quickly stripped off our clothes and jumped into bed. At this point we had been interrupted so many times by Colin and his friends that we felt a strong sense of urgency to hurry the whole thing along. It did not make for graceful lovemaking.*

We had just started kissing under the covers when the door to the bedroom swung open. It was my Mom. Rachel and I frantically pulled the covers up under our chins and clutched them tightly. We watched as she stepped into the room. Mom looked straight at me and then got a glazed look in her eyes. She wandered around the room for a minute, picking things up and putting them down. Then, without a word, she turned and walked out the door, shutting it behind her. I suddenly realized what she was doing. She was pretending to be sleep-

walking! All I could feel was a huge sense of gratitude toward her for not embarrassing us. Rachel and I looked at each other. The mood was gone. There was no way we could continue. Mom could come back at any moment.

I remained a virgin until I was 18.

COLIN

In the early 1960s our neighborhood started changing. The African Americans had crossed the invisible border at the freeway and were filling the projects across the street. At the same time the Cubans were fleeing their island home and moving into the welcoming arms of South Florida. Racial tensions were getting worse. With Sean always looking for a fight, there was no shortage of opponents. Every day there were fights of some kind.

SEAN

My teacher, Mrs. Johnson, inspired me. We were talking in class about how there were more and more Cubans coming to Florida. She said they were taking jobs and money away from us real Americans. It reminded me of how the Cubans who used to rent our duplex always seemed to have money when we didn't. I figured the government was helping them. Why didn't the government help us? We were here first and we sure needed the help. Anyhow, Mrs. Johnson said, "If you don't stand up for yourselves, those people are going to walk all over you!"

After school I started thinking about the problem. Mrs. Johnson was right, something had to be done. And then I had a brilliant idea! The blacks hated the Cubans as much as we whites did. I would call Roberto, the head of the local Cuban gang and pretend to be Jesse, the head of the local black gang. Then I'd challenge his gang to a rumble. After that I would call up Jesse, pretending to be Roberto and do the same thing. I was pretty good at faking accents, so I thought I could pull it off.

I tried my plan the next day. It was a success! I got both gang leaders so worked up that they wanted to fight immediately. The rumble was set for after school the next day.

COLIN

After school, Sean led our gang to watch the rumble at the park. There were about ten of us carrying chains, sticks, bottles, and whatever weapons we could find. We weren't sure if we were going to participate in the rumble, but it was always best to be prepared in a situation like that. We got there just as the rumble started. The two gangs stood in front of each other–about fifteen to twenty people on each side. Suddenly all hell broke loose. Chains, sticks, bottles, and rocks were flying through the air.

After a time it looked as if the black gang's stockpile of weapons was running out. "We've got to go help them!" Sean ordered. He let out a wild yell and the ten of us charged into the fray.

We swarmed toward the Cubans, flinging anything we could pick up along the way. When the Cubans saw us coming, they realized they were outnumbered and ran. Sean and Roberto had a long-standing feud so Sean took off in pursuit. Our gang followed. I tried to keep up, but I was the youngest and soon lost sight of everyone. It was time to head back to our meeting place in the cave.

I was running back through the projects when suddenly Roberto and his friend Pedro jumped out from behind a hedge and grabbed me.

"Where's your brother, little man?" Roberto demanded as he waved a huge stick at me. Pedro gripped the back of my neck with one hand and twisted my arm with the other.

"Looking for you, ya big. . .OWWWW!" I squealed as Pedro twisted some more.

"Well, I've got a message that you can give him," he said threateningly while raising the stick over his head.

Just then, the biggest black guy I've ever seen before or since grabbed Roberto's arm and Pedro's hair.

"You two best get out of this neighborhood," he roared.

Roberto dropped the stick, Pedro loosened his grip, and I fled.

I never saw The Big Black Guy again. I think he was my Guardian Angel.

COLIN

Mom just loved Martin. She'd say, "He's such a polite young boy." Or, "Martin's mama sure saw to his P's and Q's."

Martin was the same age and in the same grade as Sean, which meant he'd also been held back. But what he gave up in smarts, he made up in kindness. And big. . .that kid was BIG. He was so big that no one in school dared taunt him for hanging out with the "whities." He'd come over around dinnertime and Mom would invite him to the table–even though we didn't have a lot of extra food. He sure could eat.

One day we were hanging out in the yard not doing much of anything when Sean recalled a prank that our brother Eric used to play with his friends for entertainment. We decided we should try it ourselves. We needed a car, a pretend victim (Martin), a car full of "bad guys," and an audience. Katie's friend Trevor borrowed his Mom's station wagon and he, Sean, Dale, and I played the part of the bad guys. The audience was in a wealthy part of town where the folks spent the early evening hours sitting on porches in their rocking chairs.

Martin rode his bike along such a street. It was a nice summer night with lots of spectators in their rocking chairs. Trevor and Sean were in the front seat of the station wagon and Dale and I were in the back. We came barreling up the street toward Martin and slammed on the brakes–screeching and skidding to within inches of his bike.

BAMM! I hit the side of the car with my hand to make it sound as if we'd run into Martin. He immediately fell down and began moaning loudly–moans worthy of an Oscar. We all jumped out. I ran to the rear and opened the back door while Sean, Trevor, and Dale ran to the wailing, protesting Martin and roughly dragged him to where I waited. It took all of us to lift Martin into the back.

"Louder," Sean coaxed, and Martin poured out his soul, crying and begging us to leave him alone. While Dale and Trevor flung the bike onto the roof rack, I snuck a peek toward our audience, expecting concerned citizens to be rushing to the rescue, or at least rushing to their phones. Nobody reacted as we had hoped. They just sat in their chairs rocking away the evening.

NATIONAL GUARD CALLED IN TO QUELL RIOT

MIAMI, Aug. 8. Members of the National Guard patrolled a 250 block section of the ghetto known as Liberty City today, trying to restore order to riot-torn Miami. This is the first major racial disturbance in the city's history.

While there are conflicting stories on how the riot started, police and Negroes at the scene agree that it began Wednesday at 6 P.M., during a Vote Power rally at 1675 62nd Street. Police say that the riot started when a news reporter refused to show his identification after arriving to attend the rally. He was attacked by rally members and the violence spread out into the streets. Negroes at the scene tell a different story. They say that the presence of the police at the rally angered a group of youths who started several incidents of bottle throwing. "If ten black people get together they call it a riot, but 3000 white people can get together and they call it a convention," explained one of the Negroes present. He was referring to the Republican National Convention being held about six miles away from the riot site.

The riot escalated even further Thursday when Florida Governor Claude R. Kirk Jr. and Dade County Mayor Chuck Hall failed to show up at a promised 2 P.M. meeting for a discussion with local Negro leaders about the problems of housing, education, and jobs. The crowd of waiting 300 Negroes gathered outside the Liberty City Community Council building had an almost festive air until the Governor and Mayor failed to show up. A line of city policemen and state troopers, along with an armored riot-control truck, were lined up outside the City Council building. Someone in the crowd shouted "Why can't he get here? He can send all of his shotguns but he can't get here!" When it became apparent that the Governor and Mayor weren't coming, the crowd became angry. Some members of the crowd threw bottles at the police cars. At about 3 P.M. the police started throwing tear gas, and the riot was on again.

By the end of the day over 150 people were arrested, three Negroes were dead, and at least nine were wounded. White motorists driving home from work between 5 and 6 P.M. were dragged from their cars and beaten. A Miami police officer at the scene commented that the mobs of angry Negroes were so large that the police could not help the motorists. "All we could do was stand helplessly by," he said. Several liquor and grocery stores were looted and some fires were set. Fire trucks had to have police escorts for protection.

The police imposed a curfew from 8 P.M. to 6 A.M. and the National Guard patrolled the streets.

COLIN

It was like World War Three right in our own neighborhood! In the distant night sky we could see the fires burning. Sirens wailed and the neighborhood dogs howled in response. The National Guard rolled along our street in their yellow armored vehicles.

There was an 8 P.M. curfew in our neighborhood but we ignored it and ran through the streets hiding from any cars we saw. We wanted to get close to the action. The staging area for the National Guard was in the neighborhood park near our school. Sean, Martin, Dale, and I hid in the bushes and watched the hordes of guardsmen, policemen, and state troopers mill around. Suddenly a spotlight pointed in our direction. We ducked out of the beam and crouched among the leaves as it passed over us.

Sean said, "I think we'd better get out of here."

So following his lead, we stealthily made our way back through the neighborhood to our house.

Too keyed up to go to bed, we hung out on the front porch watching the firelight and talking. Then about a block away, we could see two carloads of yelling black men driving wildly along our street.

"Hide!" yelled Martin.

Sean, Dale, and I dived into the bushes. Martin calmly sat on the front porch watching the rowdies approach. As the two cars drove by, he casually raised his fist in the Black Panther salute. The men in the car cheered as they saluted back.

"You know," Martin said as we dragged ourselves from the bushes, "I think I should come around tomorrow and just hang out in your front yard. That way the rioters will think black people live here and leave your house alone."

And so our friend Martin protected our home from looters during the riots.

SEAN

"Sean O'Reiley, you get in here right now!" Mom yelled.

I reluctantly followed her voice into the kitchen.

"What were you thinking, coming home after midnight last night?"

"I just felt like it."

"What do you mean you just felt like it? Your curfew is 10:00 and I want you home by 10:00."

"No, I'm going to come home when I want to come home," I said defiantly.

Mom stared at me and turned to the phone. I watched with wide eyes as she dialed the number for Youth Hall and started sobbing into the receiver.

"Please, please help me! I'm sick and tired. I can't control my kid anymore. Please let me send him to you." She listened for a minute with an incredulous expression on her face.

"What do you mean you have no room? Aren't you people supposed to help me if I need it?" Mom got off the phone and wiped her eyes on her apron. She turned to me with a blank face and said. "O.K, from now on you're on your own. Just don't get caught. I give up."

COLIN

Sean and I began to run wild. Mom couldn't handle us anymore. I think she was exhausted after raising so many kids and just didn't know how to control us. She'd tried getting Youth Hall to take Sean, but they wouldn't, so she just gave up and started spending even more time in the shed behind the house with Joe, drinking vodka with beer chasers.

In the meantime, Sean and his gang of friends had discovered the joys of purse-snatching on the beach. I, the tag-along younger brother, would join them. We'd wait until someone who looked as if they had money set their towel on the sand and went into the water. Once they were far enough out into the ocean, we'd saunter over to their towel and sit on it as if it were ours. Then we'd casually go through their things. Even if the targeted people saw us, they couldn't get out of the water before we stole their money and ran. The water was always full of screaming, playing people so no one ever noticed one person was screaming about being robbed!

Sometimes the police would stake out the beach and have pretend tourists lay down towels. They were so obvious that we could always tell who they were and avoid stealing from them.

Mom never knew exactly what we were doing, but she knew it wasn't good. Some of Sean's friends were getting arrested and she was afraid that Sean would be next. One of her big fears in life was that one of her kids would go to prison. She was very proud of the fact that so far none had.

My older brother, John, was out of the Navy and living in California at the time. When he and his wife Sheri came for a visit, Mom discussed the problem with him. They decided the best thing would be for Sean to go to California to live with John and Sheri for a while. Perhaps getting him away from the influence of his friends would help keep him out of trouble.

I was filled with envy. California! What an adventure! Why couldn't I go too? I spent the day before Sean left moping and pouting around the house, sending hurt glances at Mom, John, and Sean. I was a very good pouter and it worked! Mom decided I could go along with them!

And so Sean and I moved to California when I was thirteen years old. The day after we left the police came looking for Sean. He had stolen the corner street sign to take with him as a memento and someone had seen him. Luckily, he had already left.

KATIE

I missed Colin so much. He was my best friend. I even missed mean old Sean a little. I wished they hadn't gone to California. Why did they leave me alone with Mom? At least Amy was still around.

One day Mom beat me so badly that I could barely walk. I had welts all over my legs. It was so unfair. I hadn't even done anything wrong. She had told me I couldn't go to the carnival unless I had a friend to go with. I went with Joyce, but Mom didn't believe me. She kept saying, "You're lying! You're lying! You're lying!" while she whipped my legs with a leather belt. Why didn't she believe me? I had to go to school with welts covering my legs. It hurt to walk.

I missed Colin.

SEAN

I could read! I could read! My brother John taught me to read! Mom must have told him about my problems at school and he started helping me. We read *Tom Sawyer* together and I started to figure out how to read! He read it out loud to me and I followed his finger on the page. He taught me how to sound out words. For the first time, I could answer questions in class and not feel stupid. Every day after school he helped me–page by page, line by line. He wouldn't let me have any friends over on weekdays but I didn't care–I was learning to read! He helped me with all of my homework and I finally understood it. I'll never forget how he helped me.

COLIN

"O'Reiley! Use the girl's bathroom. You can curl your hair there!"

"Yeah, girlie, we don't want you here!

"O'Reiley needs his brothers to protect him after school!"

"Scaredy-cat, scaredy-cat, little short scaredy-cat!"

The last remark was made by my most consistent tormentor, Billy Jones. I'd had enough. For weeks I had been bullied and tormented because of my long hair and short stature. The new California school was hell. The principal picked on me, the teachers picked on me, and most of the boys in my class picked on me. Only the girls seemed to like how I looked, which was a great incentive not to cut my hair! It had gotten so bad that Sean or John would walk me home from school so I wouldn't get beat up. Billy Jones and his gang never wanted to meet me one-on-one. They always seemed to bully in groups. But I'd had enough. It was time to show them how a Miami street kid could fight.

The next day I came to school with a chain wrapped around my waist. At one o'clock, the bell rang for recess and my class went outside. The school had a large park next to it and we were pretty much allowed the run of the place. There was a jungle gym, swing set, and climbing bars. I was standing near the jungle gym when Billy Jones and his gang approached.

"Hey, girlie! Want to go on the kiddy swings?"

The five boys surrounded me and started pushing me back and forth between them. All of the rage that had been building inside of me during the weeks of abuse suddenly erupted.

"GET THE FUCK AWAY FROM ME YOU BASTARDS!" (I'd learned a lot of curses from listening to my Mom.) Their jaws dropped in amazement–cursing was still relatively new to them. I whipped out my chain and started swinging it over my head.

"I'M GOING TO KILL THE NEXT BASTARD WHO TOUCHES ME! SO WHO'S IT GOING TO BE?" I started chasing Billy Jones and whipping my chain wildly at the jungle-gym, the swings, trees, anything in my way. I was a wild man full of pent-up fury. Pretty soon the gang just disappeared. I calmly wound the chain back around my waist.

From then on, I had a reputation: "He's crazy, don't mess with him!"

What the heck, I thought, *crazy runs in the family*.

KATIE

One day Mom and I were at the shopping center when we saw Flo, Dad's old girlfriend, sifting through a nearby clothes rack. Mom turned to me with mischief in her eyes.

"Watch this. I'm going to make her look like a crazy woman."

As we walked by Flo, Mom, with a huge smile on her face, very quietly said, "Bitch."

Flo immediately lost her temper and started yelling. "DON'T YOU CALL ME THAT, YOU PSYCHO LADY!"

The salesclerk, who was standing a few feet away, gave Flo a startled look.

Mom backed away from Flo, opened her eyes wide, and said, "Wha. . .what?"

"YOU KEEP YOUR FILTHY MOUTH AWAY FROM ME, YOU HEAR?"

Mom had a look of total incomprehension on her face. She said politely, "I'm sorry, I don't know what you're talking about. Do I know you?"

At this point the salesclerk was looking very nervous.

"OH YOU DEVIOUS BITCH, YOU THINK YOU CAN GET AWAY WITH THIS?"

People were stopping to stare. The salesclerk decided it was time to intervene. She turned to Flo.

"Excuse me madam, but I'm afraid I'm going to have to ask you to leave."

"ASK *ME* TO LEAVE? WHAT DO YOU MEAN ASK ME TO LEAVE? SHE STARTED IT! SHE CALLED ME A BITCH!"

Mom looked at the salesclerk and gave her a shrug of incomprehension. Then we slowly walked into another part of the store, leaving the salesclerk and Flo to fight it out. Mom started giggling.

"That Flo always did have a temper."

AMY

My ex-husband, Stuart, was shot and killed the day before my twenty-fifth birthday. We were divorced at the time and I had gone back to live with my mother and Katie.

COLIN

John was having a hard time supporting us. Mom sent him what money she could, but we never seemed to have enough. He'd been studying art and math at Berkeley but had to quit school and get a job to pay the bills. His wife, Sheri, left him. I think Sean and I helped drive her away. We tormented her whenever we could, eating like pigs in front of her and leaving messes all over the house. One time we poured a bucket full of frogs into her bed. John didn't seem to care much. I think he wanted her to leave.

We couldn't afford electricity and had very little food. Since that was how we lived back home in Florida it didn't seem unusual to us. However when I caught pneumonia, having a cold house and no food was a problem. By then I had made some friends at school and one of them, Rick, suggested that I stay with his family while I was sick. His parents kindly agreed. Soon, with good food in me and a warm bed, I started to recover.

One day Rick's little brother, Ted, was also home sick. Both of his parents had gone to work and we had the house to ourselves. We decided to play a variation of the dart game Sean used to play with me. Sean's game was to have me stand like a statue while he lobbed darts into my legs. Ted and I decided it would be more fun to chase around the house throwing darts at each other. Unfortunately we missed quite a lot of throws, and pretty soon the walls of the house were peppered with little holes. When Ted and Rick's parents came home they were not very happy with us. They figured since I was well enough to run around throwing darts, it was time for me to go back to Sean and John.

I went home the next day. When I walked in, Sean and John were whooping and hollering. Sean turned to me excitedly.

"Guess what, Colin? Eric's coming to live with us! We're going to pick him up at the airport tomorrow!"

ERIC

Mom got me into the Navy and this is the story of how she got me out.

I was waiting in Charleston for my discharge after a tour overseas when I decided to stop at a bar for a drink. Back then I had a drinking problem which had gotten me into a lot of trouble. However, it wasn't drinking that got me into trouble this time; it was love!

I thought the woman who approached me at the bar was a hustler trying to pick me up so I ignored her. I kept ignoring her until she said, "Aren't you from Miami?"

I stopped drinking my beer, took a long look at her, and said, "Yeah, how did you know?"

It turned out she used to date a friend of mine from high school. I fell in love that night. Twenty-one years old and in love for the first time. When the bar closed, I didn't want to leave her so I went AWOL. Not the brightest thing to do, thirty more days to go until I was discharged, and I decided to go AWOL. Of course, I got caught almost immediately.

I was restricted to base as a punishment, but I was obsessed with this girl. I went to see her the first chance I could get. I was allowed on a bus to go to the dentist but I decided to skip my appointment and went to her apartment. I knocked on the door.

"Who's there?" she asked.

"It's Eric!"

"Oh. . . . You can't come in!"

"Why can't I come in?"

"There's somebody here."

"What do you mean there's somebody there?"

"He's my new boyfriend."

"WHAT DO YOU MEAN YOUR NEW BOYFRIEND?"

She opened the door a little and I slammed it in. I was sober this time, but I was in full rage. I stormed through the apartment and into the bedroom. Her new boyfriend was standing across from me.

Suddenly, he pulled out a gun, a 22, and snarled "Get out of here or I'm going to blow your face off."

I looked at him and thought about it for a couple of seconds, the rage boiling inside of me. Then I shrugged my shoulders and said, "You'd better either use that gun or get the hell out of here." I started walking toward him.

He stared at me in disbelief, threw the gun down, and ran out the door.

I turned to my now ex-girlfriend and said calmly, "I left my jacket here. I'll just take it and leave."

She handed the jacket to me and I walked out the door.

I ran into her again a week before I was due to leave. I was at the transit base waiting to be shipped out. The Navy had taken me off restriction, and I decided to go out and celebrate. I went to a club that had about four hundred sailors and their girlfriends. That's where I saw them, my ex- love and her new boyfriend, having a drink and cuddling at a little table. I'd had about six or seven drinks by then. I walked over to their table and almost immediately he and I were in a fist fight. I ended it by picking up a chair and smashing it over his head.

However, as often happens in bar fights, that set off a chain reaction and pretty soon the whole bar was in an uproar! The shore patrol was called and I was hauled off and charged with inciting a riot.

By now my superior officers were pretty fed up with me, so even though I only had a week left to serve, I was facing a court martial, dishonorable discharge, and at least six months in the brig. And I'd lost the love of my life. I was pretty depressed. Then I got the news that Amy's husband, Stuart, was shot. He had been my childhood hero so this really put me into a deep depression. I snuck off the base and got drunk, which made me even more depressed.

On my way back to the barracks, I decided things were so bad I should just kill myself. I sat on a bridge that spanned some train tracks and waited for a train to come so I could jump in front of it. I waited. And waited. And waited. The beer started to wear off. I was running out of cigarettes. I was sick of waiting. I went back to my barracks and took apart one of my razors. It was about three o'clock in the morning. I went into the bathroom and stood in front of the mirror looking at myself for a long time. The first slice through my wrists was the hardest. After that I just kept going.

About ten minutes later, some poor guy opened the door to use the bathroom and saw me standing there with my wrists draining. He looked at me and looked down at the floor. There was a huge puddle of blood.

"AAAAGGGHHHHH!" He ran out and brought back four security guards.

One of the security guards was a bit of a smart-aleck. He looked at me and said, "Why don't you just slice your throat too?"

I stared at him, said, "Okay," and sliced the razor right across my throat.

At that point they realized I was serious and wrestled me to the ground.

The next morning I woke to find myself full of stitches and in the nuthouse with the guys who had freaked out from Vietnam. I felt like a complete idiot. All these guys had been in the war zone and I hadn't even seen the first sign of a war. And to top it off, now they added self-mutilation to my list of charges.

I decided to call Mom. When I told her about my suicide attempt, she started screaming, "Oh my God! Oh my God! I'll do something! Don't worry, I'll do something."

Three weeks later I was taken to the Captain. He told me all my charges were being dropped and I was going to get an honorable discharge. After three weeks in the nuthouse, I wasn't sure I was hearing him correctly.

It turned out Mom had sent a telegram to Robert Kennedy, who was Attorney General at the time, telling him the Navy was trying to kill her son–that he had tried to commit suicide, that he had done his time, and he just wanted to get out. Robert Kennedy sent a letter of inquiry to the officers at the base and after they read it, they decided to let me go. The Navy flew me to California and I will never forget how happy I was to see John, Sean, and Colin waiting to pick me up.

So I have Mom to thank for getting me into the Navy and her to thank for getting me out.

COLIN

One day Rick and I were walking home from school with three girls we wanted to impress: Molly, Kelly, and Rachel. As we strolled along, we passed a hundred-foot cliff rising out of the ground to our right. It seemed to go straight into the air.

"Hey, Rick! I bet you're too chicken to climb that!"

"*That* cliff? That's nothing! I've climbed cliffs higher than that!"

Rick threw down his books and headed for the base of the nearest rock. Not to be outdone, I followed him. Soon we were both about halfway up the cliff, with the girls watching us nervously from below.

I looked at Rick. "You know, I don't think this was such a good idea. This is steeper than I thought."

Rick nodded. "I know what you mean. Wanna go back?"

"Yeah."

We started to turn back. Rick made his way down without a problem, but I found myself frozen in place. I knew if I moved even a little, I was going to fall. It took all of my strength just to cling to the cliff wall. I couldn't move my feet even an inch. Rick and the girls started shouting up at me.

"You can do it Colin! Just go to the right a little!"

I couldn't move.

Pretty soon a whole crowd of kids from our school had gathered at the base of the cliff. I could hear them chattering and shouting below me.

"Man is he stuck. How's he going to get down?"

"Who is it anyway?"

"It's that crazy O'Reiley kid."

"What's he doing up there?"

Luckily for me a good Samaritan drove by and saw my predicament. He called the fire department and within fifteen minutes a hook and ladder truck was parked near the cliff. As I was brought down the ladder like a stuck cat, the kids below started cheering wildly. I was so embarrassed that I immediately decided to call Mom to tell her I wanted to come home.

AMY

There was something seriously wrong with Mom. It was not the alcoholism or the mental illness–it was something even worse. One morning we were sitting in the kitchen talking when she started coughing really hard into a handkerchief. I noticed something red before she hid the handkerchief.

"Mom what's that?"

"What's what?"

"Did I just see blood on your handkerchief?"

"I don't know. Maybe."

"What do you mean maybe? It's either blood or it's not."

"Yeah, it's blood."

She started coughing again. "I've seen Dr. Walton. He said I have emphysema and gave me some pills to take." She gasped and grabbed her chest, bending over in pain.

I put my arms around her shoulders and said frantically, "Mom! What is it? What's wrong?"

"Chest pains. . .I've got chest pains," she wheezed. "The doctor says it's because of the emphysema."

"Mom, Dr. Walton's a quack. I'm taking you somewhere else to get a second opinion."

COLIN

Mom and Amy scraped together enough money for me to buy a ticket home. My school sent Mom the transfer papers and I was all signed out and ready to go. That was when I realized the advantages of my situation. I had more money than I'd ever seen in my life, and the officials at the school thought I was back in Florida. Both John and Eric went to work early so they wouldn't know I was skipping school. Sean wouldn't tell on me. Why not just stick around and enjoy myself?

I developed a routine. Since I didn't own a watch, I had to be careful no one saw me during school hours. Every day when I knew it was close to three o'clock, I would hang out in a tree near the bus station. There was one nerdy kid who passed by there like clockwork on his way home from school. Once I saw him, I knew school was out and the coast was clear. I'd jump from my tree to wait for Rick at the station and we'd go off together.

My system worked great until one day I miscalculated. The nerdy kid walked by as usual, but he must have gotten out of school early. I jumped from my tree and went to the bus station to wait for Rick. A police car circled by me, but I wasn't worried since I thought school was out. The police car came by again, only this time it stopped. The officer stepped out.

"Young man, why aren't you in school?"

I looked at him in confusion but I had a reply ready.

"I go to Milton school." Milton was a new progressive school where kids were allowed to work at their own pace. Kids who went there could go home once their work for the day was done.

The officer looked at me suspiciously. "Come with me and we'll make sure you're registered there."

I climbed into the police car and he drove me to the station. When they found out I wasn't registered at *any* school, I was sent to juvenile hall for the night. Then they found out I was living with my brothers with very little supervision. After much discussion among the authorities, they decided that I had to go back home to Florida. Governor Reagan even sent my mom a letter that said something like: *We can't allow a child in our state living wild as a wolf without parental control.* I was told to go back to Florida and to stay out of California.

Right about this time we heard Mom was going to have surgery so John, Eric, and Sean decided to drive back with me to Florida.

AMY

The doctor told us Mom had lung cancer. Our world was falling apart.

KATIE

Mom lost about thirty pounds. She was so weak she couldn't get out of bed. My heart hurt every time I looked at her wide eyes full of pain. Amy and her son Evan were living with us. Amy was waiting tables at a local bar at night and sleeping whenever she could. Mom had a bell she could ring by her bed if she needed help from Amy during the day. She tried not to use it since Amy was so tired all of the time.

Amy and I divided the work between us. I had permission to come home from school every lunch period and study hall so I could make Mom's lunch and change her bedpan. Sometimes I even had to give her an enema. I babysat Evan after school while Amy cleaned the house and cooked dinner before she left for work. When Amy returned in the morning, she made us breakfast before she went to sleep.

Aunt Helen also helped out. She was a nurse's aide and worked from eleven at night to seven in the morning. She took care of her own kids during the day, but she still managed to find time to come over before and after work to give Mom her injections.

Taking care of Mom was a lot of work. Sometimes I was so tired I fell asleep with my clothes on and didn't bother changing them in the morning. But one lesson I'd learned from Mom was not to quit just because things were hard. She never gave up on us, so how could I give up on her?

Mom was in such pain and there was nothing I could do to help her. The doctor said she might get better after she had her lung removed. The boys were going to come home from California in time for the operation. I was hoping that seeing them would help Mom feel better.

COLIN

I met my Dad for the first time when I was fifteen. At least it was the first time that I really remembered. He came to visit because he'd heard Mom's operation didn't go well. The doctor said she'd feel better for a while, but the cancer was still there and she was going to die. I guess Dad thought he should come to give us some support.

It was a nice, breezy day. Katie, Amy, Sean and I were hanging out on the front porch when Mom came out and lit a cigarette. She figured since she was dying anyway she might as well keep smoking. We were all just sitting there enjoying the cool breeze when we saw Dad pull up to the curb in a large blue sedan.

Mom immediately ran into the house and locked the door. She yelled, "Don't let him in! I don't want to see him! Don't let him in! Just talk to him on the porch."

Amy thought Mom didn't want to see him because she still loved him, and she didn't want him to see her looking so ill.

Dad walked to the porch and talked to us for a while. He was still living in the Caribbean. Daniel, Amy, John and Eric had visited him there but I never had. He and Amy talked about the islands and Dad's scuba diving business for a while. He told us that when he first moved to the islands, he had asked Mom to live with him, but she didn't want to leave the states. I wondered what our life would have been like if we had moved there.

After talking for a while, Dad offered to take the four of us out to dinner. To a *real* restaurant, not just a Royal Castle! We ran into the house to tell Mom while Dad waited in the car.

On our way back out the door Mom shouted after us, "Be sure to order the most expensive things on the menu!"

When we got to the restaurant we gleefully did as she said and ordered sirloin, lobster, and all kinds of other foods we'd never eaten before. It was great!

SEAN

One day I was walking home from school when I saw an ambulance in front of our house. My heart dropped to my knees, tears started streaming down my face, and I ran as fast as I could to the front door. I thought Mom had died.

"What's wrong? What's happened?" I shouted as I rushed in.

The ambulance men were sitting by the bed holding an oxygen mask over Mom's face. Colin looked shame-faced at me.

"I gave her some chicken."

"What?"

"Well, she wanted Kentucky Fried Chicken. She kept asking for it so I bought her some."

"I can't believe you did that! You know she's only supposed to eat mushy food! You could have killed her!"

"Her food's so boring, and she really wanted the chicken. I thought just once. . . ."

"No, obviously you didn't think. So what happened?"

"Well, I fed it to her in little pieces, but she started choking. I pounded on her back but she kept choking so I called 911." Colin was crying now.

At that point, Mom pushed the oxygen mask away. "Leave him alone," she gasped. "It's my own fault, I shouldn't have asked him to do it."

I looked at Colin standing there with tears running down his face and I went over and hugged him.

AMY

My heart was breaking. For the last month all Mom had been able to do was look into my eyes and ask me when it would be over. I'd thought about ending her suffering by giving her an overdose of pain medicine, but I couldn't do it. That had to be God's decision. Then the doctor told us Mom would live only three more days. He recommended that we take her to the hospital so they could control her pain better. I wanted to do more for her, but all I could do was be with her when she died. She made me promise to make sure Sean, Katie, and Colin graduated from high school. I meant to keep that vow even if it killed me.

Katie, Sean, and Colin came to the hospital to say goodbye. One by one they went to her and held her. I couldn't stop crying. She loved her kids so much and just wanted their lives to be happier than hers was. Aunt Helen was there also. She was a rock. I don't know what we would have done without her.

The kids went home and Mom was quiet. She was squeezing my hand and looking at me with her piercing blue eyes. I didn't know if she could see me. I hoped she could. I wanted her to know that she was not alone.

"I love you Mom, we all love you so much."

She stopped breathing.

The room suddenly filled with doctors and nurses. They were rushing around the room, trying to revive her. Aunt Helen looked over at me.

"Do you want them doing this?"

I could only shake my head through the tears.

Aunt Helen went over to the doctor and said, "Let the lady die. She's suffered enough. Just let her die."

And they stopped.

SEAN

Amy was at the hospital and Katie, Colin, and I were sitting in the living room waiting for the phone call that we hoped would never come. Something caused me to look up. Above my head, there was a bright circle of light about the size of a grapefruit. With wide eyes, I watched as it slowly rose and floated across the ceiling. Twisting and turning, the circle of light flowed down the wall on the other side of the room and flew out the window that faced the church next door. I looked from Colin to Katie and back again. We knew without words what had just happened. The phone rang.

KATIE

Sean, Colin, and I were in the living room waiting for the phone call that we hoped would never come. It was starting to get dark when suddenly the lamp in the corner turned on all by itself. It went from being completely off to turning on to its highest setting. The three of us just looked at each other. Out of the corner of my eye I saw the shadow of an open book flying across the room. I heard the strum of a guitar, but there was no one near the guitar that was leaning against the wall. I remembered Mom had once told me when she died she would communicate to us through books and music. My eyes grew wide as I looked from Sean to Colin and back again. We knew without words what had just happened. The phone rang.

COLIN

Sean, Katie, and I were in the living room waiting for the phone call that we hoped would never come. A cold silence with an almost physical presence filled the room. A warm wind seemed to pass right through me. From the looks on Sean and Katie's faces, they could feel it too. The wind swirled around the room caressing everything. John's guitar sang out as it fell from a hook on the wall. A book jumped off the table, its pages ruffled by the wind. The family photograph crashed to the floor shattering glass everywhere. A get-well card took wing and twisted and turned its way around the room as if caught in a mini tornado. It slammed into the window which had its curtains stuck to the screen–pulled by the fleeing spirit wind. The whole house seemed to settle deeper on its foundation. I looked from Sean to Katie and back again. We knew without words what had just happened. The phone rang.

Our Mother had died.

EPILOGUE
Mary O'Reiley

I married Colin long after the events in this story took place. Yet stories like this never really end. I know that when I see my husband wake at night thrashing because he thinks rats are falling on his head.

What constantly amazes me about my husband's family is how well-adjusted they are. Colin's brothers and sisters don't dwell on their past but accept it for what it was. They have gone on with their lives. They have not turned into monsters. They do not use their difficult childhood as an excuse for their mistakes. They refuse to be the victims of their dysfunctional childhood.

They are normal people living normal lives.

I believe that a good deal of this is because of Marie. Her children knew she was ill, and never blamed her for the idiosyncrasies of their childhood. And in spite of considerable mental and personal problems, Marie fought with every ounce of her spirit to keep her family together, and to make them feel loved. Her one wish was that her children would finish high school. Sean, Katie, and Colin did. And now she has grandchildren who have finished college. I know somewhere she is watching them with pride.

When I asked Colin what was the most important thing he had learned from his mother, he said, "A sense of family."

And that says it all.

Suggested Questions for Book Clubs
Contributed by
The Amesbury Book Club

How would you describe Marie's raising of her children?

In today's world, Sean, Colin and Katie would very possibly be under child protection. Do you feel Sean, Colin and Katie were better off living with their Mother or child protection?

Since the author did not live this experience, do you think having each sibling tell his or her story was an effective way to tell the story?

What did you think of the children's different reactions to the same event?

Describe the different rituals the children developed to cope with their situation.

Katie wrote that Marie made their life fun. How do you think that helped the children cope later in life?

How did you react to Sean's statement about using their Cuban renters' electric power when he said, "They had a lot more money so they could afford it"?

Despite her craziness, the children were glad to have their mother home after two months with Nana. What does that say about Marie's relationship with her children?

Have you or anyone you know had an experience after-death experience similar to the one the children had on the night Marie died?

Printed in Great Britain
by Amazon

83851944R00088